OUR DAILY BREAD

JESUS SOURCE BOOK

THE A-TO-Z GUIDE TO THE PEOPLE, PLACES, AND TEACHINGS OF JESUS'S LIFE

GEORGE W. KNIGHT

Discovery House.
from Our Daily Bread Ministries

Our Daily Bread Jesus Sourcebook:
The A-to-Z Guide to the People, Places, and Teachings of Jesus's Life

Discovery House is affiliated with Our Daily Bread Ministries, Grand Rapids, Michigan.

Requests for permission to quote from this book should be directed to: Permissions Department, Discovery House, PO Box 3566, Grand Rapids, MI 49501, or contact us by email at permissionsdept@dhp.org.

Interior design by Rob Williams, InsideOutCreativeArts.com

ISBN: 978-1-62707-885-6

Printed in the United States of America
First printing in 2018

INTRODUCTION

Thousands of books have been written about Jesus Christ. So why do we need another?

Because Bible students would enjoy a quick and easy way to locate information about His life and ministry. That's what *The Our Daily Bread Jesus Sourcebook* is all about.

The true sourcebook about Jesus, of course, is the Bible, especially the four Gospels—Matthew, Mark, Luke, and John. This book does not replace the divinely inspired accounts that appear in Scripture. But *The Our Daily Bread Jesus Sourcebook* makes it easier for you to find a particular incident or detail or quotation from His ministry that you may be searching for. Just look it up in this book's handy A-to-Z arrangement of information.

Perhaps you want to find Jesus's parable of the unforgiving servant. Look under UNFORGIVING SERVANT PARABLE (page 187), where you will find a brief description of the teaching and its meaning, along with its Bible reference: Matthew 18:21–35. Now you can find the story in your own Bible, read it for yourself, and even pursue further study in other resources. This process of discovery might lead you to meditate on the parable's message—and perhaps even ask God to make you a more forgiving person in all your relationships.

Since Jesus's parables and miracles were the heart of His ministry, you will find general articles on both of these topics in this book. These overview entries contain complete lists of all His parables and miracles, handy logs to guide you to the specific article in which each parable or miracle is discussed in more detail.

In addition to these parables and miracles, *The Our Daily Bread Jesus Sourcebook* contains nearly three hundred brief articles on every aspect of His life and ministry—people He encountered, places He visited, names and titles He was known by, truths He taught, and key events such as His birth, baptism, temptation, transfiguration, crucifixion, resurrection, and ascension.

To help you search the Bible more effectively, this book also contains an extensive cross-reference system. Numerous *See* references are scattered throughout the text to help you find exactly the information you are looking for. For example, perhaps you want to search for what Jesus had to say about being born again. At BORN AGAIN, you are directed to *See* NICODEMUS (page 130). Here you will find an article on Jesus's discussion of the concept of new birth with Nicodemus, the Pharisee who approached Jesus at night. Likewise, NEW BIRTH also refers you to the Nicodemus entry. *See also* references refer you to other entries that are closely related to the subject under discussion.

Another handy feature of *The Jesus Sourcebook* is its topical index system that appears within the text itself. This index consists of sidebars on major subjects about Jesus's life and ministry. For example, see "Promises of Jesus" (page 143); listed under this topical heading are twelve individual articles from the book that pertain to His promises.

For your searching convenience, here is a list of all the subjects in this topical index feature:

My prayer is that this book, by helping you discover life-changing truths about Jesus in the Bible, will bring you closer to Him. When we get to know Him better, we will also exclaim—like those who saw Him in the flesh—"No one ever spoke the way this man does" (John 7:46).

ABBA. An Aramaic word, meaning "father," used by Jesus in His agonizing prayer in the garden of Gethsemane the night before His death (Mark 14:36).

This word shows the close relationship that Jesus enjoyed with God the Father. Most Jews of Jesus's time thought of God as a distant, unapproachable being. But to Jesus the Son, His Father was as near and dear to Him as a human father.

ABIDE IN ME. See *Remain in Me*.

ABOMINATION THAT CAUSES DESOLATION.

A prediction of Jesus that referred to the destruction of Jerusalem. This prediction came true about thirty-five years after His earthly ministry, when the city was destroyed by the Roman army (Matthew 24:15).

The phrase comes from the prophet Daniel, who predicted another calamity for the Jewish people more than five centuries before Jesus's time (Daniel 12:11). Daniel's "abomination" referred to the desecration of the Jewish temple by a pagan Syrian ruler named Antiochus Epiphanes in about 170 BC.

With His prediction, Jesus declared that another abominable event—just as bad as Daniel's prophecy—was imminent. It happened in AD 70 when the Roman general Titus put down a Jewish revolt and destroyed Jerusalem. Thousands of citizens either starved during the prolonged siege or were killed after the city fell. See also *Olivet Discourse*.

ACTS OF THE APOSTLES. A book of the New Testament
that recounts how Jesus's followers carried out the Great Commission to continue His work in the world after He ascended into heaven.

Beginning at Jerusalem, where Jesus was crucified, faithful believers witnessed among the Jewish people. But by the close of Acts, both Jews and Gentiles throughout the Mediterranean world were turning to Christianity in large numbers. A church had even been established in the capital city of the Roman Empire. This far-flung outpost of the gospel represented the fulfillment of Jesus's command to early believers to carry His message "to the ends of the earth" (Acts 1:8).

The first chapter of Acts also contains an account of Jesus's ascension into heaven after His parting commission to the apostles (Acts 1:7-11). Chapter 2 records the coming of the Holy Spirit to early believers on the day of Pentecost (Acts 2:1-4).

Throughout the first twelve chapters of Acts, the apostle Peter took the lead as a bold spokesman for the gospel. Then a zealous Jew named Saul, trying to stamp out this new faith that he considered heretical, was gloriously converted to Christianity. He soon became known as Paul, the "apostle to the Gentiles," who dominates the rest of the book. See also *Great Commission*.

ADULTERY. Engaging in sexual acts with a person other than your spouse. This sin is prohibited by the seventh of the Ten Commandments (Exodus 20:14). The law of Moses specified that a person committing adultery should be stoned to death (Leviticus 20:10).

In Jesus's day, a group of Pharisees and teachers of the law once brought to Him a woman accused of adultery. They asked Jesus what He had to say about her sin, reminding Him of the Old Testament command to stone adulterers, hoping to trap Jesus into making a statement they could use against Him.

But Jesus turned the table on the woman's accusers. "Let any one of you who is without sin," He declared, "be the first to throw a stone at her" (John 8:7). Jesus was saying that judgment against sin is best left in God's hands, that only those who are free of sin can sit in judgment over the sin of others.

Every one of the woman's self-righteous critics walked away, shamed by Jesus's wisdom and grace. Then He assured the woman that He didn't condemn her, but at the same time He issued a challenge: "Go now and leave your life of sin" (v. 11). Jesus offered no easy forgiveness that demanded nothing of the woman—she had to decide between her old way of life or the way of righteousness as a follower of Jesus.

In His broader teachings on adultery, Jesus also warned against sexual lust and unbridled desire. Filling one's mind with fantasies can lead to the physical act of adultery itself, so He warned, "Anyone who looks at a woman lustfully has already committed adultery with her in his heart" (Matthew 5:28).

ADVOCATE. A title of Jesus expressing the idea that He pleads for His followers before God the Father (1 John 2:1).

All believers, though redeemed by God's grace, have moments when they fall into sin. When this happens Jesus intercedes on their behalf with God the Father. When Christians confess their sins, He restores them to a right relationship with a holy and righteous God.

Jesus has the right credentials to represent His people when they are accused of wrongdoing because of His atoning work as Savior through His death on the cross.

AENON. A place where John the Baptist continued to baptize converts after he had baptized Jesus (John 3:23). Aenon's exact location is unknown today, though it was along the upper reaches of the Jordan River. It was near Salim, another site with a location lost to history.

Probably neither Aenon nor Salim was the site of Jesus's baptism. He was apparently baptized in the lower reaches of the Jordan River, in the desert area near the Dead Sea. This is the region where John was preaching when Jesus launched His public ministry (Luke 3:1-9). See also *Baptism of Jesus*; *Bethabara*.

AKELDAMA. See *Field of Blood.*

ALPHA AND OMEGA. A name of Jesus that emphasizes His completeness, eternity, and oneness with God the Father (Revelation 1:8). Alpha is the first letter of the Greek alphabet, and Omega is the last. Thus, this name declares that Jesus is the beginning and the end—the first and the last—and everything in between.

He existed with God the Father as the agent of creation before time began (John 1:3). He brings meaning to His people's day-to-day existence. And He gives believers hope for the future when their earthly lives come to an end. Jesus is the eternal one in whom people can place their total trust.

ANDREW. One of the original twelve disciples, or apostles, of Jesus. According to the gospel of John, he was the first of the apostles (1:40-42). Andrew was a follower of John the Baptist before he became Jesus's disciple.

Almost every time Andrew is mentioned in the Gospels, he is bringing someone to Jesus. After meeting Jesus, he found his brother Peter and introduced him to the Master (John 1:41). At the feeding of the five thousand, Andrew told Jesus about the boy whose lunch was multiplied to feed the hungry crowd (John 6:8-9). As the Lord's earthly ministry was drawing to a close, Andrew—along with Philip—told Jesus about a group of Greeks who wanted to talk with Him (John 12:20-22).

Andrew and his brother Peter were fishermen from the coastal village of Bethsaida on the Sea of Galilee (John 1:44). See also *Disciples of Jesus.*

ANGELS. Spiritual beings who serve as special messengers of God and as agents of His power in the world. Angels are created beings—thus not divine—but they are superior to humans in knowledge and strength.

Angels played a special role in the life and ministry of Jesus. The angel Gabriel announced to the virgin Mary that she would give birth to "the Son of the Most High" (Luke 1:32). In the last book of the New Testament, Jesus confirmed that He had sent the angel who shared the visions that the apostle John recorded (Revelation 22:16).

Angels also:

- Told Zechariah that his son, John, would prepare the way for the Messiah (Luke 1:11–17);

- Announced Jesus's birth to shepherds (Luke 2:9–14);

- Warned Joseph in a dream to flee to Egypt (Matthew 2:13);

- Told Joseph when to return to his home country (Matthew 2:19–20);

- Ministered to Jesus after His temptations ended (Matthew 4:11);

- Rolled away the stone that sealed Jesus's tomb (Matthew 28:2);

- Appeared to several women at the empty tomb (Matthew 28:5) and individually to Mary Magdalene when she lingered at the tomb (John 20:11–12);

- Will accompany Jesus at His return (Matthew 16:27) and sound trumpets in the end time (Matthew 24:31).

ANNA. An elderly prophetess who recognized the infant Jesus as the Messiah when He was dedicated at the temple in Jerusalem (Luke 2:36–38).

Anna's husband had died after they had been married for only seven years, and she had been a widow for many years after that. But this tragedy didn't make her bitter or resentful—she worshiped and prayed in the temple every day. Her faithfulness was rewarded by a glimpse of the babe-in-arms who was the long-awaited Messiah.

Anna passed on this good news to many other people "who were looking forward to the redemption of Jerusalem" (verse 38).

ANNAS. A Jewish religious official before whom Jesus appeared after His arrest (John 18:12-13). A former high priest of the Jews, Annas may have insisted that Jesus be brought to him because of a personal grudge.

Jesus had driven merchants and moneychangers out of the temple (Matthew 21:12-13). This shady business enterprise may have been operated by Annas and his family.

After questioning Jesus, Annas sent Him to the current high priest, Caiaphas, to be tried before the Jewish Sanhedrin (John 18:24). Caiaphas was Annas's son-in-law. See also *Caiaphas*.

ANNUNCIATION OF JESUS'S BIRTH. The formal proclamation to the virgin Mary that she would give birth to Jesus, the Messiah. This message was delivered by the angel Gabriel just a few months after he had announced the birth of John the Baptist to Zechariah and Elizabeth (Luke 1:26-38).

An annunciation of a different type was made to Joseph, the man who had promised to take Mary as his wife. When it became apparent that she was pregnant, Joseph determined to break his marriage pledge. But an angel informed him that Mary's pregnancy was supernatural and that she would give birth to the Messiah. This divine reassurance convinced Joseph to proceed with the marriage (Matthew 1:18-25). See also *Mary, Mother of Jesus*; *Virgin Birth*.

ANOINTING OF JESUS. One of two lavish displays of love for Jesus which occurred at different points in His earthly ministry. Both actions were performed by women who poured expensive perfume on His feet, then wiped them with her hair.

The first anointing happened early in Jesus's ministry when a sinful woman approached Him in the home of Simon the Pharisee. Jesus contrasted the woman's act of love and devotion with the cold reception He had received from Simon. The Lord rewarded her faith by extending forgiveness for her sins (Luke 7:36–50).

The second anointing occurred just a few days before Jesus's ministry on earth came to a close. Three gospels record this event, but only John's reveals that the woman was Mary of Bethany, sister of Lazarus (John 12:3–8; see also Matthew 26:6–13; Mark 14:3–9).

Judas, the disciple who later betrayed Jesus, objected to what he considered a waste of costly perfume. But Jesus commended Mary's unselfish act, describing it as a form of preparation for His approaching death. "It was intended that she should save this perfume for the day of my burial," He declared (John 12:7). See also *Mary, Sister of Lazarus*; *Simon the Pharisee*.

ANTICHRIST. An evil being who opposes Christ (*anti* means "against") and His work in the world. The word does not appear in the Gospels, but is prominent in the additional writings of the apostle John.

According to John, many antichrists were already at work during the latter years of the first Christian century. He identified them as false teachers, many of whom denied the divinity of Jesus (1 John 2:18–23), while others insisted that He did not exist in a human body (1 John 4:2–3). John affirmed in his gospel that Christ was both fully human and fully divine (John 1:1–14).

In John's book of Revelation, he envisioned the rise of a single evil being of great power in the end time. This antichrist, "the beast," will war against Christ and the forces of good. But he and his henchman, the false prophet, will be defeated and "thrown alive into the fiery lake of burning sulfur" (Revelation 19:20). See also *Satan*.

ANTIPAS. See *Herod,* No. 3.

APOSTLES. See *Disciples of Jesus.*

APPEARANCES OF JESUS AFTER HIS RESURRECTION. According to the book of Acts, the period between Jesus's resurrection and His ascension lasted for forty days (1:3).

His followers were slow to believe that Jesus had broken the bonds of death, so He spent time with them to prove that He was still alive. During these forty days, He also prepared them to continue His work on earth through the church by relying on the power of the Holy Spirit (Acts 1:4–8).

The four Gospels record several appearances of Jesus to His followers during this period. In the book of 1 Corinthians, the apostle Paul also mentioned several post-resurrection appearances of Jesus that do not appear in the Gospels. According to these sources, Jesus appeared:

- to Mary Magdalene at the empty tomb (John 20:11–18);
- to another woman named Mary, along with Mary Magdalene, at the empty tomb (Matthew 28:1–10);
- to two followers on their way to Emmaus, a town not far from Jerusalem (Luke 24:13–32);
- to Peter, apparently in Jerusalem (Luke 24:33–35);

- to ten of His disciples in Jerusalem at a time when Thomas was not present (John 20:19–25);
- to the eleven disciples, including Thomas, in Jerusalem a week later (John 20:26–29);
- to His disciples at the Sea of Galilee (John 21:1–14);
- to His disciples at His ascension near Jerusalem (Luke 24:44–53);
- to more than five hundred followers (1 Corinthians 15:6);
- to James and all the apostles (1 Corinthians 15:7); and
- to the apostle Paul (1 Corinthians 15:8). Paul was probably referring to his dramatic vision of Jesus on the road to Damascus, an event that resulted in his conversion to Christianity (Acts 9:1–19).

ARCHELAUS. See *Herod,* No. 2.

ARIMATHEA. See *Joseph of Arimathea.*

AFTER THE RESURRECTION

Acts of the Apostles

Appearances of Jesus after His Resurrection

Ascends into Heaven

Emmaus

Firstborn from Among the Dead

Great Commission

Lord's Day

Mary Magdalene

Miraculous Catches of Fish

Resurrected from the Grave

Thomas

ASCENDS INTO HEAVEN. After His earthly ministry came to a close, Jesus returned to God the Father. The event was witnessed by the eleven disciples who remained with Jesus after the suicide of the betrayer, Judas.

Jesus was "taken up" from the Mount of Olives (Acts 1:9), near the village of Bethany (Luke 24:50-51). After He disappeared into a cloud, two angels assured the disciples that His return was just as certain as His dramatic return to God the Father.

The supposed site of Jesus's departure is marked by two different churches—the Catholic Chapel of the Ascension and the Russian Orthodox Church of the Ascension. Both are visited by pilgrims to the Holy Land.

ASK, AND YOU WILL RECEIVE. A promise of Jesus to His disciples (John 16:24). He admitted that He would no longer be with them in the body, but they could continue to draw strength for the days ahead through the presence and power of the Holy Spirit.

The key to this promise is the little word *ask*. Many people who need help are too proud to request assistance. Followers of Jesus admit their shortcomings and ask Him to keep them growing both in their commitment to Him and in their service as citizens of His kingdom.

ASK, SEEK, KNOCK. See *Sermon on the Mount*, No. 6.

ASSOCIATES WITH SINNERS. After Jesus called Matthew as His disciple, the tax collector hosted a meal to which he invited his tax collector friends to eat with the Lord. Also present were many other people who were classified as "sinners" by the scribes and Pharisees. They criticized Jesus for associating with such people (Luke 5:27-32).

To the religious establishment of Jesus's time, "tax collectors and sinners" were those who did not keep the rituals and requirements of the Jewish law. They were unclean people—the outcasts of society—who would defile anyone who associated with them.

But Jesus treated such people with respect and compassion. He showed by His acceptance that God welcomed all people who were willing to turn to Him. To the criticism of the scribes and Pharisees He responded, "I have not come to call the righteous, but sinners to repentance" (verse 32). The self-righteous fault-finders actually paid Jesus a great compliment when they accused Him of being "a friend of tax collectors and sinners" (Matthew 11:19).

ATONEMENT. The restoration of a spirit of harmony between God and humankind. This unity was broken by Adam and Eve in the garden of Eden when they sinned by disobeying God's clear command (Genesis 3:1-6). Through Jesus's atoning death on the cross, He reversed the curse of sin and made it possible for sinful humans to be reconciled to God.

This restoration occurs when people repent of their sin and place their faith in Jesus as God's agent of redemption (Romans 3:21-26).

AUGUSTUS. See *Caesar Augustus.*

AUTHOR AND PERFECTER OF FAITH. A title of Jesus that challenges believers to follow His example of courage and endurance. Not only did He serve as author, or creator, of our faith, He brought it to perfection—that is, completion (Hebrews 12:2 NASB).

Jesus never wavered from the mission that He came into the world to accomplish. He persevered all the way to the cross,

giving us a perfect example of what it means to live the life
of faith.

The NIV translates the word *author* in this passage as
"pioneer." Through His perfect obedience and atoning death,
Jesus blazed a trail that leads believers to joyful fellowship
with God the Father.

AUTHORITY OF JESUS. The right of Jesus to teach
spiritual truths and perform miracles through divine power—
an authority that came from God the Father (John 5:26-27).

The common people of Jesus's time were quick to recognize
His validity as a teacher and miracle worker. They were amazed
by His teachings because He taught on His own authority
(Matthew 7:28-29).

Jesus connected with these people by using down-to-earth
analogies and figures of speech from everyday life that they
could easily understand. His approach was a welcome change
from the dull, stilted style of the teachers of the law, who quoted
from other experts to support their teachings.

This openness toward Jesus and His teachings did not extend
to the Jewish establishment. The chief priests, elders, and teachers
of the law rejected His authority, probably because He was not a
member of their exclusive circle (Mark 11:28-33).

The supreme insiders known as the Pharisees were even
more skeptical of Jesus's claim to act with God's authority.
When He healed a paralyzed man and forgave his sins, they
wondered, "Who can forgive sins but God alone?" (Mark 2:7).
They were blind to the reality that God in human flesh was
standing among them.

BAPTISM OF JESUS. The event that marked the beginning
of Jesus's public ministry. For thirty years Jesus had lived and
worked with His family in the village of Nazareth. News that His
forerunner, John the Baptist, was declaring that the kingdom

of God was at hand must have been the sign that it was time for the Messiah's work to begin (Luke 3:21-23).

Jesus submitted to John's baptism of repentance, although He had no sins of which to repent. In this act, Jesus declared that He approved of John's ministry and would continue to call people to turn from their sins and become citizens of the kingdom of God. Through His own baptism, Jesus identified with the sinful people He came to save.

As John performed the baptismal rite, the Holy Spirit descended on Jesus. Then God the Father spoke in a loud voice, "This is my Son, whom I love; with him I am well pleased" (Matthew 3:17). All three persons of the Trinity—Father, Son, and Holy Spirit—indicated that a wonderful work of God was about to begin through the life and ministry of Jesus. See also *Bethabara; John the Baptist.*

BARABBAS. A notorious criminal whose release was requested by the crowd when Jesus appeared before Pilate, Roman governor of Judea. The governor often set a prisoner free during the Passover celebration to curry favor with his Jewish subjects.

Pilate's offer to free either Jesus or Barabbas was an attempt to avoid executing Jesus, whom the governor believed to be innocent. But the crowd foiled his plan when they called for Jesus's crucifixion and Barabbas's release (Matthew 27:15-23).

Barabbas was a murderer who had been involved in a Jewish uprising against the Roman government (Mark 15:7-11). The irony of this episode is that a criminal who challenged the authority of Rome was set free, but an innocent man was condemned to a brutal death on a Roman cross.

BARREN FIG TREE CURSED.

See *Curses Barren Fig Tree.*

BARREN FIG TREE PARABLE. Jesus told a parable about a fig tree that had never produced a single fig. The land-owner ordered the tree to be cut down. But the owner's servant wasn't ready to give up. He convinced the owner to wait one year to see if it could be nurtured into a productive tree (Luke 13:6–9).

In Jesus's mind, this useless fig tree represented the nation of Israel. God had given the Jewish people every opportunity to represent Him before the other nations of the world. But they had grown arrogant and proud of their heritage, refusing to show God's love and acceptance to the Gentiles.

Now, through the ministry of Jesus, God was giving the Jews a final chance to become fruitful for the Lord. If they continued in their sin and pride, they would be cut down from their privileged position as God's chosen people. See also *Curses Barren Fig Tree.*

BARTHOLOMEW. See *Nathanael.*

BARTIMAEUS. See *Blind Bartimaeus Healed at Jericho.*

BEATITUDES. The eight declarations of blessedness made by Jesus at the beginning of His Sermon on the Mount (Matthew 5:2–12). The word comes from a Latin term that means "blessed" or "content." These statements portray the state of bliss or satisfaction that belongs to those who are committed to Jesus and the principles of the kingdom of God.

Those who are especially blessed by God include "the poor in spirit," those who realize their need for Him; those who mourn over their sins; the meek, who are humble and free of pride; those who thirst for the righteousness that comes only from God; those who show mercy to others, just as God has been merciful to them; the pure in heart, who are totally devoted to

God; the peacemakers, who work to reconcile people with one another and with God; and those who endure persecution and hostility from others because of their commitment to Jesus and His teachings. See also *Sermon on the Mount.*

BEELZEBUL. A name for Satan, the prince of demons, that Jesus's critics used to try to discredit His ability to heal those who were demon-possessed (Mark 3:22).

The demented people whom Jesus restored to their right minds were indisputable proof of His healing power. So His critics charged that He was performing these miracles through the power of Satan.

Jesus answered these claims with a bit of logic: How could He cast out demons through the power of the master demon? This would mean that Satan was divided against himself, frustrating his own purposes. Satan wanted to control people through evil spirits, not free them. So, Jesus declared, His power to heal came from none other than God the Father (Luke 11:20). See also *Demons and Demon Possession; Satan.*

BELOVED DISCIPLE. See *John the Apostle.*

BENEDICTUS. The song of praise offered by Zechariah the priest after his son, John the Baptist, was born (Luke 1:67-79). The title comes from the Latin word for "blessed," with which the song begins in the NKJV. Zechariah praised God for choosing John as the one who would prepare the way for the coming of the Messiah. See also *Zechariah.*

BETHABARA. A place on the Jordan River where John the Baptist was preaching when Jesus sought to be baptized (John 1:28 KJV).

DISEASE AND DISABILITY

Blind Bartimaeus Healed at Jericho

Blind Man Healed at Bethsaida

Centurion's Servant Healed

Deaf Man with Speech Impediment Healed

Demons and Demon Possession

Lame Man Healed on the Sabbath

Leprosy

Man Born Blind Healed

Man with Body Fluid Healed

Man with Deformed Hand Healed

Paralyzed Man Healed

Peter's Mother-in-Law Healed

Royal Official's Son Healed

Two Blind Men Healed

Woman with Hemorrhage Healed

Most modern translations of the Bible render the Greek word for Bethabara as *Bethany.* But this is a different place than the Bethany near Jerusalem where Lazarus and his two sisters lived.

The reputed site of Bethabara is on the Jordanian side of the Jordan River, across from the nation of Israel. Jordanian officials claim Bethabara is the place where Jesus was baptized by John the Baptist, but the exact place where this occurred is uncertain. See also *Baptism of Jesus.*

BETHANY. A village near Jerusalem where Jesus raised His friend Lazarus from the dead (John 11:1–44). During His trips to Jerusalem, Jesus often visited in the home of Lazarus and his two sisters at Bethany.

This is where Jesus corrected Lazarus's sister, Martha, because she was too busy in the kitchen to spend time listening to His teachings (Luke 10:38–42). According to Luke's gospel, Bethany is also the site where Jesus blessed

His disciples before ascending into heaven after His resurrection (Luke 24:50–51).

The reputed site of the raising of Lazarus is marked today by a Catholic shrine known as the Church of Saint Lazarus. Not far away is a dark, underground cavern that has been revered for centuries as the cave where Lazarus's body was entombed until Jesus shouted, "Lazarus, come out!" (John 11:43). See also *Lazarus Raised from the Dead*.

BETHESDA. See *Pool of Bethesda*.

BETHLEHEM. A village about six miles south of Jerusalem where Jesus was born (Luke 2:1–7), in fulfillment of Old Testament prophecy (Micah 5:2). The manger in which Jesus was placed by His mother, Mary, was a feeding trough for livestock. This makeshift cradle reflects the humble circumstances of His birth.

The reputed spot of Jesus's birth is located in a cave inside an ancient church known as the Church of the Nativity. This fortress-like building is one of the most sacred sites in the Christian world. It has stood on this site in the middle of the town for more than sixteen hundred years.

Not far away is another shrine connected with Jesus's birth: the Milk Grotto. This is said to be the place where Mary and Joseph hid their son from the soldiers who carried out King Herod's death order against all the male babies born near Bethlehem (Matthew 2:16–18). The shrine is named for the milk that supposedly dropped on the floor while Mary was nursing the infant Jesus.

Just outside Bethlehem is a plot of ground known as Shepherd's Fields. This is revered as the place where angels announced "good news of great joy" to shepherds who were tending their sheep on the night Jesus was born (Luke 2:8–10).

Bethlehem is also known as the "city of David" because it was the hometown of the shepherd boy who grew up to become the greatest king of Israel (Luke 2:4).

BETHPHAGE. A village from which Jesus launched His triumphal entry into Jerusalem (Matthew 21:1–3). The site of this town is unknown, but tradition places it on the Mount of Olives just outside Jerusalem.

A Catholic chapel known as the Church of Bethphage marks the reputed site of the town. The church contains a painting of Jesus on a donkey as He rode into the Holy City. See also *Triumphal Entry into Jerusalem*.

BETHSAIDA. Hometown of three of Jesus's disciples: Andrew, Peter, and Philip (John 1:44; 12:21). These three made their living as fishermen on the nearby Sea of Galilee.

At this village Jesus healed a blind man by rubbing saliva on his eyes (Mark 8:22–26). But in spite of His miracles in and around Bethsaida, most residents were skeptical of His ministry. He condemned the town for its unbelief (Luke 10:13).

Recent excavations have confirmed that Bethsaida was indeed a center of the fishing trade during Jesus's earthly ministry. Archaeologists have discovered several tools used by fishermen of that era.

BETRAYAL OF JESUS. See *Judas Iscariot*.

BIRTH OF JESUS. More than six hundred years before Jesus was born, the prophet Micah predicted that the Messiah would come into the world in Bethlehem, a village just a few miles from Jerusalem (Micah 5:2). One of the great ironies of history is that this prophecy was fulfilled through the decree of a pagan king.

B

Caesar Augustus, emperor of the Roman Empire, ordered a census throughout the lands under his rule so all citizens could be taxed. Obeying these orders, Joseph took his fiancée Mary with him to register at Bethlehem, his ancestral home. She was carrying in her womb the baby who had been conceived by the supernatural action of the Holy Spirit. While in Bethlehem, Jesus was born in a stable, the only accommodations available in the crowded town (Luke 2:1-7; see 1:26-33).

Shepherds from the surrounding fields came to welcome this newborn into the world after angels had startled them with the news. Then these "lowly people" of the working class spread the word to others about what they had seen and heard—thus becoming some of the first witnesses to proclaim that the Savior of the world had been born (Luke 2:8-20). See also *Bethlehem*; *Caesar Augustus*.

BLASPHEMY. The act of dishonoring, disrespecting, or showing contempt toward God, an offense that was punishable by death under the Old Testament law.

Jesus's enemies accused Him of blasphemy for several reasons—for forgiving people of their sins (Luke 5:21), for identifying himself as the promised Messiah (Mark 14:61-64), and for claiming to be God (John 10:33). Blasphemy was the charge brought against Him by the Sanhedrin, the Jewish high court (Matthew 26:65).

Even though the Sanhedrin convicted Jesus of this crime, the Roman authorities would not allow the Jews to carry out the death sentence. So the Jewish court sent Jesus to Pilate, who condemned Him to death on the charge of leading a rebellion against Rome (John 19:12-16).

BLASPHEMY AGAINST THE HOLY SPIRIT. A serious sin that Jesus attributed to the Pharisees when they accused Him of casting demons out of people through the power of Satan,

B

or Beelzebul (Matthew 12:22-32). Jesus went on to say that this sin "will not be forgiven" (verse 32), thus designating it as an affront to God sometimes referred to as the "unpardonable sin."

One interpretation of this passage holds that the Pharisees' sin was just what the Bible says: attributing the work of God to Satan and his evil influence. But the verse can also refer to a broader sin—persistently rejecting Jesus as the Savior He claimed to be. People who continue to reject Him never admit their sin, see no need to repent, and thus remain in spiritual darkness, and unforgiven.

BLESSED IS HE WHO COMES IN THE NAME OF THE LORD. A shout of the crowd when Jesus made His triumphal entry into Jerusalem (Matthew 21:9). Jesus also used this phrase in reference to himself when He predicted His second coming (Matthew 23:39). See also *Triumphal Entry into Jerusalem*; *Second Coming*.

BLESSES LITTLE CHILDREN. See *Children Received by Jesus*.

BLIND AND DEAF MAN HEALED. See *Demons and Demon Possession*, No. 6.

BLIND BARTIMAEUS HEALED AT JERICHO. Bartimaeus couldn't see, but he could hear. And as he sat by the road begging for handouts, the clamor of the crowd told him that Jesus was passing through (Mark 10:46-52).

Bartimaeus knew about this miracle worker from Galilee who had healed others, so he shouted to get His attention. *Perhaps this is my lucky day,* he may have thought, *and Jesus might take pity on me as He passes through.*

When the crowd tried to silence Bartimaeus, he shouted even louder. Then Jesus called him over and restored his sight—right on the busy road, filled with travelers on their way to Jerusalem for the annual Passover celebration.

Jesus knew that this trip to Jerusalem would be His last. But His compassion compelled Him to take notice of a desperate blind man among the crowd. It was one of the last miracles Jesus performed during His public ministry.

BLIND LEADING THE BLIND. A saying of Jesus that condemned the Pharisees for their lack of spiritual leadership (Matthew 15:1-14). As the major religious party of the time, the Pharisees were known for their fierce devotion to the externals of the law—avoiding contact with sinners, eating only certain foods that were considered clean, and the ritualistic washing of the hands before eating.

But Jesus taught that such practices had nothing to do with one's worthiness before God. What mattered was not observing burdensome laws but keeping one's heart pure and undefiled in obedience to God.

In Jesus's view, the Pharisees were blind to spiritual truth—and they were leading the common people to accept the same false view of religion. "If the blind lead the blind," He declared, "both will fall into a pit" (verse 14). See also *Pharisees*.

BLIND MAN HEALED AT BETHSAIDA. Jesus and His disciples were traveling toward Caesarea Philippi, about twenty-five miles north of the Sea of Galilee. At the town of Bethsaida they were met by a group of people leading a blind man. They begged Jesus to heal this man of his disability (Mark 8:22-26).

Jesus led the man outside the town away from the crowd, perhaps to keep him from being agitated and confused by curious spectators. Then Jesus rubbed His saliva on the man's sightless eyes to begin the healing process. At first the blind man could make out only faint images. But Jesus touched his eyes again, and he could see everything clearly.

B

This healing is the only miracle recorded in the Gospels that took place in two distinct stages. Some interpreters speculate that Mark included it to send a subtle message: just like the blind man who gradually regained his sight, the disciples were slow to come to a complete understanding of Jesus and His mission in the world.

BOANERGES. See *Sons of Thunder.*

BODY OF CHRIST. See *Head of the Church.*

BORN AGAIN. See *Nicodemus.*

BOTTLE. See *Wineskin.*

BOYHOOD OF JESUS. See *Childhood of Jesus.*

BOY WITH SEIZURES HEALED. See *Demons and Demon Possession,* No. 2.

BREAD OF LIFE. A title of Jesus that pictures Him as the spiritual sustainer of His people. He used this title for himself after He multiplied a few pieces of bread and a couple of fish to feed a hungry crowd in the wilderness (John 6:1–59).

In a long teaching session, Jesus used the imagery of bread several times to show that He provided the spiritual nourishment that people needed. He was the bread of God (verse 33), the bread of life (verse 35), and the living bread (verse 51).

Bread made from wheat or barley was the staple of Bible times, so the common people could identify with this imagery. They knew that bread also played a prominent role in the pivotal event of Jewish history—the exodus from Egypt. The Lord delivered His people from slavery so hurriedly that they baked their bread without leaven, or yeast, because they didn't have time to let the bread rise (Exodus 12:17-20). While they traveled in the wilderness toward their new home in Canaan, the Lord kept them alive by providing manna, a bread substitute (Exodus 16:4-5; 31-32).

In declaring himself to be the living bread, Jesus called to mind all these recollections of bread from the past. Regular bread provides nourishment for a little while, but those who eat the spiritual food He provides will never hunger. See also *Feeds Five Thousand People; Feeds Four Thousand Gentiles.*

BRIGHT MORNING STAR. A name of Jesus comparing Him to the star that continues to shine in the eastern sky after other stars disappear at daybreak (Revelation 22:16). To the ancients, this lingering heavenly light was known as the morning star. Modern astronomers believe it was actually the planet Venus, Earth's closest neighbor in the solar system.

Just as Venus remains visible at sunrise, marking the beginning of a new day, so the birth of Jesus ushered in a new era for humankind. He offers all believers the joy of salvation and the hope of eternal life.

BROTHERS OF JESUS. Jesus was born to Mary, a young virgin, through the supernatural action of the Holy Spirit. But He had four brothers who were later born to Mary and her husband, Joseph, through natural means. These brothers—more accurately half brothers—were James, Joseph, Judas, and Simon (Mark 6:3).

During Jesus's earthly ministry, His brothers were skeptical of Him and His work as a wandering teacher and healer (John 7:5). On one occasion they tried to force Him to return home to

DOCTRINES OF CHRIST

Atonement

Authority of Jesus

Fulfillment of the Law

Fullness of Time

Head of the Church

Humanity of Jesus

"I Am" Statements of Jesus

Immanuel

Incarnation of Jesus

Kingdom of God

Lord's Supper

Mediator

Offices of Christ

Preexistence of Jesus

Take Up One's Cross

Universal Reign of Jesus

Virgin Birth

Nazareth with them because they thought He was out of His mind (Mark 3:21).

At least one brother, though, James, changed his attitude and became a believer after Jesus's death and resurrection. James emerged as a leader of the church in Jerusalem (Acts 15:12-19; 21:17-18), and is believed to be the author of the epistle of James in the New Testament. Jesus's brother Judas (or Jude) may also have been active in the early church—some scholars believe he was the author of the New Testament's epistle of Jude.

Jesus also had sisters, but their names are not mentioned in the Gospels (Matthew 13:56; Mark 6:3).

BURIAL OF JESUS. See *Joseph of Arimathea.*

BURIED TREASURE. See *Kingdom of God Parables.*

CAESAR AUGUSTUS. Emperor of the Roman Empire at the time Jesus was born. This political leader issued a decree for a taxation census that resulted in Joseph traveling with Mary to Bethlehem (Luke 2:1-4). Here Jesus was born in fulfillment of an ancient prophecy (Micah 5:2). This is a perfect example of how God uses human circumstances—even pagan rulers—to work out His purpose.

This "Caesar Augustus" is probably the emperor known to historians as Octavian. He ruled over Rome for almost half a century, until his death in AD 14. See also *Roman Empire*.

CAESAREA PHILIPPI. A town about twenty-five miles north of the Sea of Galilee where the disciple Peter confessed Jesus as the Messiah (Matthew 16:13-20).

Jesus may have deliberately chosen this place as the site where Peter would make his great confession. Caesarea Philippi had been associated with pagan worship for many centuries. In Old Testament times, it was a center of Baal worship. In Jesus's time, a shrine devoted to the Greek nature god known as Pan was located here.

Still visible today is a hollowed-out space in the cliffs above the site of the ancient town, where statues of pagan gods once stood. Here Peter confessed Jesus as the Messiah, the son of the living God—a distinct contrast to these dead gods of the past.

The site of ancient Caesarea Philippi is known today by its Arabic name, Banias. From this high place at the foot of Mount Hermon, a spring flows south to join other springs to form the headwaters of the Jordan River. See also *Peter*.

CAIAPHAS. The high priest of the Jews who plotted the arrest of Jesus (Matthew 26:3-4) and presided over His trial by the Sanhedrin. Caiaphas and the other members of this group declared that Jesus deserved to die for the crime of blasphemy (Matthew 26:57-66).

The office of high priest had apparently been passed on to Caiaphas by his father-in-law, Annas. Some time before Jesus was arrested, Caiaphas had declared that Jesus deserved to die for the crimes of blasphemy and rebellion against Roman authority (John 11:45-53). This strong accusation was probably a political move by the high priest to curry the favor of the Roman government.

Archaeologists have discovered an ornate tomb near Jerusalem that bears the name Caiaphas. This has led some scholars to wonder if this could be the burial site of the very man before whom Jesus appeared. See also *High Priest; Trials of Jesus.*

CALMS A STORM. Early in His ministry, Jesus got into a fishing boat with His disciples to cross the Sea of Galilee. Tired from a day of teaching the crowds, He soon fell asleep in the rear of the boat. This is a perfect picture of His humanity: He grew exhausted just like any person who had worked hard all day long (Mark 4:35-41).

While Jesus was resting, a sudden storm threatened to swamp the small craft and the disciples woke Him up with desperate cries that they were about to die. Now the divine side of His nature took control. Jesus gave a brief command to the howling wind and the churning water: "Quiet! Be still!" (verse 39). Immediately the wind died down and the raging waves grew totally calm.

Jesus gently chided the disciples for their weak faith in this perilous situation. Why had they been petrified with fear when the Master over the storm was right there in the boat with them? All they had to do was ask for His help.

The disciples murmured to one another, "Who is this? Even the wind and the waves obey him!" (verse 41). They realized for the first time that this Jesus they followed was more powerful than the force of nature itself.

Generations of believers have found in this account a clear and inspiring message: no matter what troubles we experience, through Jesus we find calm in the midst of the storm. See also *Walks on the Water.*

CALVARY. See *Skull, The.*

CANA. A town in the region of Galilee where Jesus performed His first miracle—turning water into wine (John 2:1-11). The village was about six miles northeast of Nazareth, Jesus's hometown.

Cana is the site of a church known as the "Wedding Church" that was built to commemorate this miracle. Another nearby church is named for Jesus's disciple Nathanael, who lived at Cana (John 21:2). See also *Turns Water into Wine.*

CAPERNAUM. A town on the northern shore of the Sea of Galilee where Jesus lived during His Galilean ministry (Matthew 9:1; Mark 2:1). It was a logical base for His work, since four of His disciples—Peter, Andrew, James, and John—were from Capernaum (Mark 1:16-21). A fifth disciple, Matthew, apparently was a tax collector in the town (see Luke 5:27-32).

At Capernaum and throughout the surrounding area, Jesus performed many of His healing miracles (Mark 1:21-28; 2:1-5). He lived here for about two years, although He had grown up at Nazareth, about twenty miles away.

Jesus's disciple Simon Peter had a house at Capernaum. Jesus healed Peter's mother-in-law at this residence (Matthew 8:14). The reputed remains of this house are viewed today by Holy Land visitors through the glass floor of a shrine known as the Octagon Church.

Another sacred spot near Capernaum is Tabgha, the traditional site of the feeding of the five thousand. A church known as the Church of the Multiplication commemorates this miracle.

In spite of Jesus's work in and around Capernaum, many people rejected Him and His message. He condemned the town for its unbelief (Matthew 11:23).

CARPENTER. A derogatory term used to describe Jesus by the citizens of His hometown of Nazareth (Mark 6:3). See also *Joseph, Husband of Mary.*

CENTURION'S SERVANT HEALED. A group of Jewish officials approached Jesus, asking Him to heal the servant of a local Roman army officer. This man was a centurion, an accomplished commander who led a detachment of about a hundred foot soldiers (Luke 7:1-10).

As Jesus set out to find the servant, the centurion sent Him a personal message. He told Jesus, in effect, "You don't even have to come into my house. Just stand outside and give the command, and my servant will be healed."

This Roman officer realized that most Jews would not enter the house of a Gentile like him. But he believed Jesus had the power to heal at a distance. The Lord was amazed at such faith from a pagan foreigner, because so many of His own people refused to believe in Him. Jesus honored this show of faith by restoring the centurion's servant to health.

CEPHAS. See *Peter.*

CEREMONIAL WASHING. The Pharisees and teachers of the law believed that people were defiled by touching impure things, eating unclean foods, or even being in a public place where sinners were present. This defilement, they thought, kept them from being acceptable to God. The antidote for such uncleanness was ceremonial washing—taking a prescribed bath or scrubbing the hands up to the elbows in an elaborate cleansing ceremony.

A group of these religious leaders charged Jesus and His disciples with breaking tradition by not washing their hands in ritualistic fashion before they ate (Matthew 15:1-11). Jesus responded by telling the gathered crowd: "What goes into someone's mouth does not defile them, but what comes out of their mouth, that is what defiles them" (verse 11). He went on to explain to His disciples that impure things that come from the heart, including lust, a vengeful spirit, and evil thoughts, are the true source of defilement.

This principle is one of the most important in the teachings of Jesus. What matters in religion is not keeping the right rules and observing the proper rituals but keeping the heart pure before the Lord.

CHIEF CORNERSTONE. See *Cornerstone.*

CHIEF PRIESTS. Leaders of the priestly hierarchy who opposed Jesus and His work. These religious leaders questioned His authority (Matthew 21:23), instigated His arrest (Mark 14:43), mocked Him on the cross (Matthew 27:41), and directed Pilate to make sure His tomb was sealed and secure (Matthew 27:62-65).

These chief priests were often allied with the elders of the people in opposition to Jesus (Matthew 26:3-4). These elders were apparently leaders of well-known Jewish families who exercised some influence in the religious and political life of the nation.

CHILDHOOD OF JESUS. Little is known about Jesus's growing-up years, though bizarre accounts of His childhood appear in some early writings that are considered inauthentic. The gospel writers apparently considered these years of little significance, focusing instead on His life after Jesus reached adulthood and launched His public ministry.

Luke's gospel contains the only recorded event from Jesus's childhood (2:41-52). His parents were on their way back to Nazareth after a visit to Jerusalem, where they had celebrated

C

the annual Jewish Passover. Realizing their twelve-year-old son was missing, Joseph and Mary returned hurriedly to the Holy City. There they found Him in the temple, discussing religious questions with noted Jewish teachers.

This was not a one-way conversation dominated by a precocious boy. Jesus was sitting quietly among these experts, "listening to them and asking them questions" (verse 46). He was anxious to learn from their fertile minds.

Mary scolded Jesus for lagging behind and creating anxiety for His family. He replied, "Didn't you know I had to be in my Father's house?" (verse 49). This answer shows that, from an early age, He had some understanding of His unique mission as God's Son. But years of questioning, testing, and seeking were needed before He was fully ready for the task. So Jesus returned home willingly with His parents to continue to grow "in wisdom and stature, and in favor with God and man" (verse 52).

CHILDREN RECEIVED BY JESUS. It was a common practice in Jesus's time for a noted rabbi or religious teacher to place his hands on infants and bless them on their first birthday. This is what happened in the familiar story of Jesus and the children—mothers brought their babies to Him to receive His blessing (Luke 18:15-17).

The disciples wanted to turn the mothers away, probably because they thought Jesus was too busy to bother with such a trivial matter. But Jesus welcomed the children, took them in His arms, and blessed them (Mark 10:16). He also used them to teach an important spiritual lesson: "Anyone who will not receive the kingdom of God like a little child will never enter it," He declared (verse 15).

To Jesus, children modeled the traits of openness and acceptance that were essential for those who would become His followers. Like these little ones, believers must be trusting, obedient, and eager to forgive.

CHORAZIN. A town near the Sea of Galilee that Jesus condemned for its refusal to accept Him and His message (Matthew 11:21). The Gospels do not contain any record of His teaching and healing at Chorazin. But He must have done so many times, since the town was just a stone's throw from Capernaum, the center of His Galilean ministry.

A tourist attraction known as Korazim National Park sits on the site today. Here archaeologists have uncovered the remains of a ritual bath, an olive press, several houses, and a Jewish synagogue.

CHRIST. A name for Jesus that means "anointed one," referring to the Messiah expected by the Jewish people. See also *Messiah*.

CHURCH. See *Head of the Church*.

CLEANSES THE TEMPLE. A day after Jesus's triumphal entry into Jerusalem, He returned to the city. The Passover celebration was still underway, and Jerusalem was filled with people who had traveled long distances to attend this national Jewish festival.

Jesus grew angry when He noticed the outer courtyard of the temple being used as a marketplace. So He drove away the merchants who were selling animals and other items for use in sacrificial rituals. He also overturned the tables where money exchangers were offering their services (Mark 11:15–17; *moneychangers:* KJV). They were probably exchanging foreign coins of the Passover pilgrims for the correct coins needed to pay the Jewish temple tax.

The religious officials of Jerusalem may have been involved in these transactions for their own personal profit. Jesus quoted from the prophet Isaiah, "My house will be called a house of prayer" (Isaiah 56:7), and accused these merchants of defiling the temple: "But you are making it a 'den of robbers'" (Matthew 21:13).

Many Bible students are puzzled about when this event actually occurred. John's gospel places Jesus's cleansing of the temple near the beginning of His public ministry (John 2:13-17). But Matthew, Mark, and Luke record it as happening during His final week in Jerusalem, just before He was crucified. Were these the same event, or two separate cleansings of the temple?

It's impossible to know for sure. But the gospel of Mark is clear about the result of this action of Jesus: the Jewish religious establishment could not ignore this bold challenge to its authority, and the leaders "began looking for a way to kill him" (Mark 11:18). See also *Temple*.

CLEOPAS. A follower of Jesus who interacted with the resurrected Christ without recognizing Him on the day of resurrection. Jesus talked with Cleopas and another traveler while

THE END TIMES

they walked to their home in Emmaus, seven miles from Jerusalem. Not until Jesus came into their house and broke bread with them did they recognize Him as the risen Lord (Luke 24:13-32). See also *Emmaus*.

COMMISSION. See *Great Commission*.

COMMUNION. See *Lord's Supper*.

COMPASSION OF JESUS. The emotional response of Jesus to people who were suffering pain and loss. This trait of His character is evident throughout His public ministry. A careful study of the Gospels reveals that He was deeply moved by several different circumstances that He encountered among people.

1. **Hopelessness.** Many of the common people among whom Jesus moved were longing for a satisfying relationship with God, but their religious leaders offered them only a dry system of rules and regulations. The scribes and Pharisees were fastidious law-keepers themselves, and they looked upon those who could not or did not comply as sinners and outcasts.

When Jesus saw this situation, he was moved with compassion for the ordinary people because "they were harassed and helpless, like sheep without a shepherd" (Matthew 9:36). He recognized that legalistic religion was nothing but a burden, and He offered the people rest and hope if they would place their faith in Him (Matthew 11:28).

2. **Sorrow.** As Jesus and His disciples entered the village of Nain, they were met by a funeral procession. The group was leaving the town to bury the only son of a widow (Luke 7:11–17). When Jesus saw the woman crying, "His heart went out to her" (verse 13), and He raised the young man from the dead and presented him to his mother.

Centuries before Jesus arrived on earth in human flesh, the prophet Isaiah predicted that He would be "a man of sorrows, and acquainted with grief" (Isaiah 53:3 KJV). It's comforting to know that He understands our sorrow and is there to comfort us in our times of grief.

3. **Disabilities and afflictions.** In a sense, all of Jesus's healing miracles were a result of His compassion for people. But one situation in which His compassion is specifically mentioned occurs in Matthew's gospel. Two blind men were sitting by a road begging for handouts when the clamor of the crowd told them that Jesus was passing by. They called out to Him to have mercy on them. Moved by their condition, Jesus touched their eyes and restored their sight (Matthew 20:29–34). He was especially moved by those who suffered from physical disabilities.

CONFESSION OF JESUS BY PETER. See *Caesarea Philippi; Peter.*

CONSIDER THE LILIES. A phrase from Jesus's Sermon on the Mount that assures believers of His constant love and care. God takes care of wildflowers, Jesus emphasized, and He will certainly provide for those who devote their lives to Him. See also *Sermon on the Mount,* No. 4.

CORNERSTONE. A title of Jesus that emphasizes His role as the bedrock of the Christian faith (Matthew 21:42; *head of the corner:* KJV). In constructing the stone structures of Bible times, tradesmen used a cornerstone to strengthen two walls where they were joined together.

Jesus is the unmovable force on which our faith is based. He is the source of our strength when we are struck by the tragedies and tribulations of life. We are safe in the storm when we depend on Him as our refuge and strength. As the psalmist declared, "My soul finds rest in God; my salvation comes from him. . . . He is my fortress, I will never be shaken" (Psalm 62:1-2).

C

COUNCIL. See *Sanhedrin.*

COUNSELOR. See *Wonderful Counselor.*

CREATOR. See *Alpha and Omega.*

CROSS BEARING. See *Take Up One's Cross.*

CRUCIFIXION OF JESUS. Jesus was charged with the crime of inciting rebellion against the Roman government. On this false charge, He was sentenced to die by crucifixion on a Roman cross. This form of capital punishment was noted for the suffering it caused its victims.

All four gospels contain accounts of the crucifixion. Jesus was placed on the cross at the third hour, or about 9:00 in the morning (Mark 15:25). He died at the ninth hour, or about 3:00 in the afternoon (Luke 23:44-46), after about six hours on the cross. This quick death was a result of God's mercy, since crucifixion victims sometimes lingered in agonizing pain for several days (John 19:31-33).

In addition to physical pain, Jesus also suffered mental and emotional anguish on the cross. He was mocked and taunted by Roman soldiers, religious officials, and curious onlookers in the crowd (Matthew 27:39-44). He was humiliated by having a crown of thorns placed on His head as a mockery of His claim to be a king (Matthew 27:29).

Perhaps Jesus's greatest emotional trauma was the feeling that He had been abandoned by God the Father in these hours of suffering and despair. He expressed this feeling by quoting these words from Psalm 22:1: "My God, my God, why have you forsaken me?" (Matthew 27:46). That must have been the moment when the One who knew no sin took the sins of the whole world upon himself (2 Corinthians 5:21). The collective penalty that He paid for sinful humankind was a feeling of separation from God which sin always creates in the human heart.

The onlookers around the cross must have been startled when an ominous midday darkness that lasted for three hours fell over the scene (Luke 23:44). This may have signified that nature itself was horrified at the cruelty and suffering to which Jesus was being subjected. Or perhaps the darkness was a sign of Satan's attempt to destroy the Son of God.

To the Jewish people, crucifixion was a shameful way to die (Galatians 3:13). But Jesus transformed the cross into a symbol of unselfish love and God's amazing grace. See also *Death of Jesus*.

CRY OF DERELICTION. See *Seven Sayings from the Cross*, No. 5.

CUP OF SUFFERING. Jesus's imagery for the painful death that He faced on the cross (Luke 22:42). In the Old Testament, the prophet Jeremiah spoke of the cup of upheaval and disaster that awaited God's people unless they turned from their idolatry (Jeremiah 25:27–29). Jesus may have alluded to this symbol to show that He needed to drink the cup of suffering to become the agent of redemption for a sinful world. See also *Gethsemane*.

CUP OF WATER. An image used by Jesus that shows the value of even the smallest act of service performed in His name. He assured His disciples, "Anyone who gives you a cup of water in my name because you belong to the Messiah will certainly not lose their reward" (Mark 9:41).

People who are front and center in Christian ministry—preachers, evangelists, teachers—usually receive praise and recognition for their efforts. But Jesus reminds us that the simplest acts of ministry, such as showing hospitality and kindness to others, are just as important in the work of bringing people into God's kingdom.

CURSES BARREN FIG TREE. This action of Jesus, recorded in Mark 11:12–14, 20–21 and Matthew 21:18–22, has caused endless difficulties for interpreters. Why would Jesus curse a fig tree for not bearing fruit when it was not the season for ripe figs?

One possible answer is that this incident is a continuation of Jesus's parable of the barren fig tree. The meaning of the parable was that the nation of Israel had failed to bear fruit for the Lord. When Jesus saw this fig tree, it had green leaves and offered the promise of ripe fruit in a few weeks. But its potential was still unfulfilled. So Jesus condemned it to show that God's patience with Israel as His witness to the world had come to an end. See also *Barren Fig Tree Parable.*

CYRENE. See *Simon of Cyrene.*

CYRENIUS. See *Quirinius.*

DALMANUTHA. See *Magadan.*

DAUGHTER OF A GENTILE WOMAN HEALED. See *Demons and Demon Possession,* No. 3.

DEAF MAN HEALED. See *Demons and Demon Possession,* No. 5.

DEAF MAN WITH SPEECH IMPEDIMENT HEALED.

When Jesus was in the Decapolis, a Gentile territory near the Sea of Galilee, some people brought to Him a deaf man who could hardly speak. They begged Jesus to heal this unfortunate man (Mark 7:31–37).

Jesus took the man away from the crowd, possibly to prevent his embarrassment. Then He put His fingers in the deaf man's ears and placed His saliva on the man's tongue. These gestures were a type of sign language, signifying that Jesus was about to open the man's ears and unbind his tongue. Saliva was considered a healing agent by some cultures of Jesus's time.

Next, Jesus looked to heaven to show that His power to heal came from God. When He uttered the word *ephphatha,* an Aramaic term meaning "be opened," the man could hear sounds and he began to speak clearly.

This miracle amazed the crowd. To avoid creating a public spectacle, Jesus told the people not to talk about what had happened. But they could not contain their excitement as they declared, "He even makes the deaf hear and the mute speak" (verse 37).

DEATH OF JESUS. Three supernatural events or signs occurred at Jesus's death (Matthew 27:50–54). These signs point to several significant truths about the atoning death of Jesus.

1. **Tearing of the curtain in the temple.** This curtain separated the holy of holies from the rest of the temple in Jerusalem. Only the Jewish high priest could enter the area beyond this barrier, and he did so only once per year on the day of atonement. In this sacred space, the high priest first made atonement for his own sins and then the sins of the people. The mysterious split of this curtain from top to bottom at Jesus's death declared that all

people now had access to God through the person of His Son.

2. **Earthquake.** This sudden shaking of the earth symbolized nature's disapproval of the cruelty and injustice of Jesus's execution. This jolt from the hand of God may have caused the split of the curtain in the temple.

3. **Opening of graves.** The earthquake also caused the tombs of many holy people to break open. Then, after Jesus was resurrected, these "saints" (KJV) returned to life and came out of their graves to appear "to many people" (verse 53). This event appears only in Matthew's gospel. Matthew probably included it to show that those people who had died before Jesus's atoning death would be included in God's kingdom and His promise of bodily resurrection and eternal life. See also *Crucifixion.*

DECAPOLIS. A district with a large Gentile population where Jesus healed a demon-possessed man who lived among the tombs.

THE FINAL WEEK OF JESUS

Bethphage

Blessed Is He Who Comes in the Name of the Lord

Cleanses the Temple

Farewell Address to His Disciples

Feast of Passover

Greeks Ask to See Jesus

Holy Week

Jerusalem

Judas Iscariot

Lord's Supper

Olivet Discourse

Trials of Jesus

Triumphal Entry into Jerusalem

Upper Room

Washes the Disciples' Feet

People throughout this territory were amazed when the man told them about his miraculous healing (Mark 5:1-20). In this area Jesus also performed the miracle of feeding a crowd of four thousand Gentiles (Matthew 15:29-38).

The name *Decapolis* means "ten cities." These cities, including Gadara (Matthew 8:28) or Gerasa (Mark 5:1), were centers of Greek culture and tradition from days gone by. This pagan influence continued into New Testament times. See also *Gentiles*; *Feeds Four Thousand Gentiles*.

DEDICATION FEAST. See *Feast of Dedication*.

DEMONS AND DEMON POSSESSION. A careful study of the Gospels reveals that Jesus had a special concern for people who were under the control of demons—also referred to as "impure spirits" (Matthew 10:1; *unclean spirits:* KJV).

Some Pharisees in Jesus's time claimed they had the power to cast evil spirits out of people (Matthew 12:27). But they did so through elaborate rituals and magical incantations. Jesus simply ordered demons to leave people. This showed that He was master over Satan and his evil forces.

In addition to the general statement that Jesus healed "the demon-possessed" (Matthew 4:24), the Gospels record His healing of seven specific persons who suffered from this affliction.

1. **Wild man among the tombs.** In Gentile territory, Jesus and His disciples met a violent man who lived among the tombs in a cemetery. He was possessed by several demons—an entire legion, the man admitted to Jesus. These demons sensed that Jesus had the power to cast them out, so they begged Him to let them enter a nearby herd of pigs. Jesus honored this request, and the pigs drowned when they rushed into the waters of the Sea of Galilee (Mark 5:1-20).

Some people wonder why Jesus would cause the destruction of a herd of innocent animals. But it's clear that He wasn't the cause; He simply allowed it to happen. And besides, wasn't the restoration of this miserable man to a full and meaningful life worth more than two thousand pigs?

2. **Boy with seizures.** When Jesus came down from the mountain where He had been transfigured, He found His disciples in a dispute. A group of scribes was ridiculing Jesus's followers because they had been unable to heal a demon-possessed boy who was deaf and suffered from epileptic seizures (Mark 9:14-29).

Jesus first rebuked the disciples for their lack of faith. He had delegated to them the ability to heal (Mark 3:14-15), but they had not drawn on the power that could have made this poor boy well.

Then Jesus turned His attention to the boy's father. Did he believe that Jesus could heal his son? The man's response was a mixture of faith and doubt: "I do believe," he declared, "help me overcome my unbelief" (verse 24). At this reply Jesus cast the evil spirit out of the boy and presented him to his father.

Later the disciples asked Jesus privately why they had failed to cast out this demon. He replied, "This kind can come out only by prayer" (verse 29). Constant prayer—cultivating our relationship with Jesus day by day—is the key to keeping His power active in our lives.

3. **Daughter of a Gentile woman.** Jesus was in Gentile territory near the coastal cities of Tyre and Sidon, northwest of the Sea of Galilee—the greatest distance He ever traveled outside Jewish territory. Here, away from the clamor of the crowds, He planned to relax and spend some important time teaching His disciples (Matthew 15:21-28).

But His reputation as a healer and teacher had preceded Him, even to this distant place. A woman approached Jesus, pleading with Him to heal her demon-possessed daughter. At first Jesus ignored the woman's request. Then, after her persistent begging, He told her, "It is not right to take the children's bread and toss it to the dogs" (verse 26).

Jesus was acting out the attitude of the Jewish people toward all non-Jews, whom they referred to as Gentiles. The Jewish people thought of these foreigners as "dogs" who did not deserve God's love. But the woman's reply—that even dogs deserved to eat the crumbs that fell from the table—was what Jesus wanted to hear. He commended her great faith and healed her daughter.

The disciples learned an important lesson that day: no nationality or ethnic group has an exclusive claim on God's love. Jesus was sent into the world as the Savior of *all* people.

4. **Man in the synagogue.** Jesus was teaching in the synagogue at Capernaum when He was interrupted by a loud cry. A demon inside a man in the audience recognized Jesus, called Him by name, and begged Him to go away (Luke 4:31-35). The demon apparently recognized that Jesus had the power to break his grip on this unfortunate man. Jesus immediately commanded the demon to come out. With a loud shriek (Mark 1:26), the evil spirit obeyed and left the man.

5. **Deaf man.** This man was unable to hear or speak. As soon as Jesus cast his demon out, he was able to speak clearly. This amazed the common people, but the Pharisees claimed that Jesus was performing these healing miracles through the power of Satan (Matthew 9:32-34). Even miracles do not convince people who are blinded by their unbelief.

6. **Blind and mute man.** This man had multiple disabilities—blindness, an inability to speak, and demon possession—and could not find Jesus on his own. So a group of his friends brought him to Jesus. Immediately the master healer restored him to health (Matthew 12:22-24).

This healing is similar to that of the demon-possessed deaf man (see No. 5 above). Some scholars believe these two accounts describe the same event. But since both appear in Matthew's gospel, they are best interpreted as two separate events. Jesus's healing of both men resulted in a charge by the Pharisees that He was healing through the power of Beelzebul, the prince of demons (Matthew 9:34, 12:24).

7. **Woman with crooked back.** Jesus was teaching in the synagogue on the Sabbath when He noticed a woman with a

severe curvature of the spine (Luke 13:10-17). She had suffered for eighteen years from being "crippled by a spirit" (verse 11), apparently a reference to her possession by demons.

Jesus placed His hands on the woman, and she straightened up immediately and began praising God. The ruler of the synagogue was indignant with Jesus over this act of healing, believing He had broken the law against working on the Sabbath. Jesus replied that farmers were allowed to untie their oxen and take them out of their stalls to be watered on the Sabbath. Wasn't it appropriate, then, that this unfortunate woman should be set free from Satan's grip on the Sabbath?

8. **Mary Magdalene.** According to Mark's gospel (16:9), Jesus had cast seven demons out of Mary Magdalene, although no details about this event are recorded in the Gospels. See also *Mary Magdalene.*

DENIAL OF JESUS. See *Lord's Supper.*

DEVIL. A name or title that Jesus often used for Satan (Matthew 13:39; Mark 7:29 KJV). **See also** *Satan.*

DIDYMUS. See *Thomas.*

DISCIPLES OF JESUS. The twelve followers selected by Jesus to learn from Him and to continue His work after the ascension. These disciples are also referred to as apostles—people sent by Jesus on a special mission.

Jesus probably selected exactly twelve disciples because of the importance of this number in the history of the nation of Israel. The children of the patriarch Jacob had evolved into the twelve tribes of Israel.

Some of these disciples are mentioned only a time or two in the Gospels, while others have a more prominent role in Jesus's ministry. For example, Peter, James, and John appear with Jesus at significant points in His ministry, such as His transfiguration (Luke 9:28-36) and His agonizing prayer in the garden of Gethsemane (Mark 14:32-36). For this reason, these three are often referred to as the "inner circle" of His disciples.

Lists of the twelve disciples appear in the gospels of Matthew (10:2-4), Mark (3:14-19), and Luke (6:13-16), as well as in the book of Acts (1:13-14). The names in these lists are not exactly the same; differences exist because several of the disciples had more than one name.

Here is a composite list of the Twelve, with their different names listed and a brief description of each. For more information, see each name at its appropriate location in this book.

1. **Peter (Simon Peter):** A fisherman from Galilee; brother of Andrew.

2. **Andrew:** A fisherman from Galilee; brother of Peter.

3. **James:** A fisherman from Galilee; son of Zebedee; brother of John.

4. **John:** A fisherman from Galilee; son of Zebedee; brother of James.

5. **Philip:** From Bethsaida.

6. **Nathanael (Bartholomew):** From Cana in Galilee.

7. **Thomas (Didymus):** Perhaps a fisherman.

8. **Matthew (Levi):** A tax collector from Capernaum.

9. **James:** Son of Alphaeus; also known as James the less or James the younger.

10. **Thaddaeus (Judas, son of James):** Called Judas, son of James to distinguish him from Judas Iscariot, the disciple who betrayed Jesus.

11. **Simon (Simon the Zealot):** He was associated with Jewish revolutionaries known as the Zealots, known for their opposition to the Roman government.

12. **Judas Iscariot:** From Kerioth in southern Judah; the disciple who betrayed Jesus.

See also *Matthias*.

DISCIPLES SENT OUT. See *Sends Out His Followers.*

DISCIPLE WHOM JESUS LOVED. See *John the Apostle.*

DIVINITY OF JESUS. See *Immanuel; Mediator; Virgin Birth.*

DIVORCE. See *Marriage and Divorce.*

DONKEY. See *Triumphal Entry into Jerusalem.*

DOOR FOR THE SHEEP. See *Good Shepherd.*

DROPSY. See *Man with Body Fluid Healed.*

EGYPT. See *Flight into Egypt.*

ELDERS OF THE PEOPLE. See *Chief Priests.*

ELI, ELI, LAMA SABACHTHANI. See *Seven Sayings from the Cross,* No. 5.

THE FIRST CHRISTMAS

ELIJAH. A fiery Old Testament prophet to whom Jesus compared John the Baptist (Matthew 17:10–13; *Elias:* KJV). Jesus made this comparison to three of His disciples after His transfiguration. At this event, Moses and Elijah appeared and talked with Jesus (Mark 9:2–8).

In Old Testament times, Elijah was known as a great miracle worker. And he never experienced death since he was taken into heaven in a whirlwind (2 Kings 2:11). Some Jews believed the prophet would come back to earth and continue his ministry of miracles, which is probably why some people thought Jesus himself was Elijah (Matthew 16:13–14). Jesus's mighty works reminded them of the old-time miracle worker.

ELIZABETH. A relative of the virgin Mary, mother of Jesus. After Mary discovered she would give birth to the Messiah, she paid a visit to Elizabeth, who was also pregnant. Elizabeth was carrying the baby who would grow up to become John the Baptist, forerunner of Jesus.

When Elizabeth greeted Mary, the baby stirred noticeably in Elizabeth's womb—a mysterious response of the unborn forerunner to the imminent arrival of the unborn Messiah. Elizabeth then rejoiced with Mary over the coming birth of the Son of God (Luke 1:39-45). See also *Zechariah*.

EMMAUS. A village not far from Jerusalem where Jesus appeared to two followers just a few hours after His resurrection. One of these believers was Cleopas; the other, although unnamed, could have been his wife (Luke 24:13-35).

The two were walking from Jerusalem to their home in Emmaus late on resurrection Sunday when Jesus joined them on the road. For some reason they did not recognize Him. This is dramatic proof that no one—not even Jesus's closest followers— expected Him to rise from the dead, although He had told them clearly that this would happen.

When they reached their home in Emmaus, the two invited their traveling companion to come inside and eat with them. After Jesus gave thanks for the meal, He broke the bread and handed it to them, and they suddenly recognized Him as the risen Lord. Then Jesus disappeared. The two believers rushed back to Jerusalem to tell the disciples the exciting news.

The site of Emmaus has never been identified. Though Luke says it was seven miles from Jerusalem (24:13), no one knows in which direction. See also *Cleopas*.

ENTRY INTO JERUSALEM. See *Triumphal Entry into Jerusalem*.

ESAIAS. See *Isaiah*.

ESCHATOLOGICAL DISCOURSE. See *Olivet Discourse.*

EUCHARIST. See *Lord's Supper.*

EVIL ONE. See *Satan.*

E

EXPERT IN THE LAW. A religious official who had mastered the Old Testament law and took pride in telling others how to apply the law to every life situation. Jesus often clashed with these experts by doing things which they considered unlawful, such as healing people on the Sabbath (Luke 14:3; *lawyer:* KJV).

Jesus condemned these experts because they had added thousands of explanations and commentaries to the written law contained in the five books of Moses, what Christians now consider the beginning of the Old Testament. They considered these additions as authoritative as the original Scriptures. Jesus told them with a note of sarcasm, "You have a fine way of setting aside the commands of God in order to observe your own traditions!" (Mark 7:9).

These religious officials are often referred to in the Gospels as teachers of the law (Matthew 23:23). Another name for them in the King James Version is scribes (Mark 7:1).

EYE FOR EYE. A phrase from Jesus's Sermon on the Mount that represented the teaching of the Old Testament law. A person who had lost an eye through a blow from another person was allowed to destroy one of his assailant's eyes in retaliation (Exodus 21:22–24).

But Jesus overturned this law. He taught a higher ideal known as non-retaliation (Matthew 5:38–40). Citizens of God's kingdom should resist the temptation to "get even." They should show restraint and even kindness toward those who do them wrong.

Humanly speaking, this type of behavior is impossible. Only through God's strength and the presence of the Holy Spirit can we resist the natural impulse to strike back when we suffer wrong and injustice.

But Jesus was clear that believers are expected to cultivate this attitude in all human relationships. He declared, "Love your enemies and pray for those who persecute you" (Matthew 5:44). Notice that these words require something from us—prayer. The best way to conquer our bitterness and our tendency to strike back is to pray for those who do us wrong. See also *Sermon on the Mount*.

E

F

EYE OF A NEEDLE. See *Zacchaeus*.

FALSE CHRISTS. See *Olivet Discourse*.

FAREWELL ADDRESS TO HIS DISCIPLES. In a

lengthy monologue at the Lord's Supper, Jesus expressed His love for His disciples and bade them a fond farewell. This passage, which appears only in John's gospel, is one of the longest speeches of His public ministry (John 14:1–16:33).

Although Jesus would soon leave His disciples in a physical sense, He assured them of His continuing influence and inspiration through the Holy Spirit. This supernatural power and presence would continue the work of the kingdom of God through His chosen disciples, other followers, and the church He was establishing.

Jesus sensed that the disciples were anxious about His leaving, so He calmed their anxiety with the promise, "My peace I give you" (John 14:27). He did not promise His followers that they would be free from conflict, according to the world's definition of peace. But they would enjoy a calmness of spirit in spite of the troubles they might face. They didn't need to be afraid because they had Jesus's promise of His continuing presence.

Jesus also reminded the Twelve that their lives should be filled with love for one another. He had loved them fondly, and after His ascension to the Father, they should continue to love one another. The disciples' unselfish love would bring joy to God the Father and His Son, Jesus, who was the ultimate example of sacrificial love.

Finally, Jesus wanted to prepare His disciples for future hardships they would face as His witnesses. If they remained faithful to Him, they would be persecuted just as He had been during His public ministry. After all, Jesus declared, "a servant is not greater than his master" (John 15:20). But in spite of these earthly troubles, the disciples would experience joy if they remained faithful to Jesus and the divine truths He had taught them. See also *Holy Spirit*.

FEAST OF DEDICATION. An eight-day Jewish festival or holiday that celebrated the restoration of the temple during the Maccabean revolt about 150 years before Jesus's time. He attended at least one of these celebrations in Jerusalem (John 10:22–39).

During this festival the religious leaders challenged Jesus to tell them openly whether He was the long-awaited Messiah. A positive answer would give them grounds to accuse Him of blasphemy. But Jesus avoided their trap: rather than answer yes or no, He invited them to consider the miraculous works He was performing in the name of God the Father.

The Jewish people today still celebrate this festival. Known as the Festival of Lights or Hanukkah, it may occur from late November into late December, depending on the lunar cycles of the Jewish calendar.

FEAST OF PASSOVER. The major national Jewish festival that was being celebrated in Jerusalem when Jesus was crucified (Matthew 26:1–2). This event commemorated the Lord's deliverance of the Israelites from Egyptian slavery in the days of Moses (Exodus 12:21–27).

This holiday was called the Passover because the Lord "passed over" the homes of the Israelites while striking dead the firstborn children in every Egyptian home. This was the tenth and final plague the Lord sent to convince the pharaoh of Egypt to release the Israelite slaves.

Jesus's crucifixion during this celebration had special significance for His early followers. To them His death was like the sacrifice of a lamb that was eaten at a special meal during the Passover commemoration. In his writing the apostle Paul referred to Jesus metaphorically as "our Passover lamb" (1 Corinthians 5:7).

This celebration went on for several days, during which the Jews ate unleavened bread. This custom recalled the fact that the Israelites left Egypt so suddenly that they did not have time to add leaven to their dough (Exodus 23:15). Thus, the event is sometimes referred to as the Feast of Unleavened Bread. See also *Lamb of God*.

FEAST OF TABERNACLES. A major Jewish festival that celebrated God's provision for His people in the wilderness after their deliverance from slavery in Egypt. Jesus's skeptical half brothers attended this annual celebration in Jerusalem, and they taunted Him to come along with them and perform miracles for the crowds that would be gathered in the Holy City.

Jesus refused to join them, but after they left He traveled to Jerusalem by himself. This was His way of declaring that He never performed miracles just to create a spectacle, to excite the crowds, or to call attention to himself (John 7:1–10).

Jesus did not perform a single miracle at the festival; He spent His time teaching the people and talking with the religious leaders about the nature of His work as a messenger sent from God. He waited until the very last day of this eight-day festival to declare openly who He was and what He had come to earth to do.

On this final day, historians tell us, a priest would pour water on the altar in the temple, symbolizing the water that God had miraculously provided for His people in the wilderness. At this moment Jesus declared that He had been sent from God the Father as living water to quench the spiritual thirst of a sinful world (John 7:37-39).

F

FEAST OF UNLEAVENED BREAD. See *Feast of Passover.*

FEEDS FIVE THOUSAND PEOPLE. This miracle of Jesus has the distinction of being the only one recorded by all four gospels. It happened when He and His disciples tried to escape the crowds by slipping away to a remote place near the Sea of Galilee. But the people followed, bringing the sick and disabled for Him to heal (Luke 9:10-17).

Late in the day, Jesus had compassion on the people because they were hungry and had nothing to eat in this isolated place. One of the disciples, Andrew, discovered a boy in the crowd who had brought a meager lunch. Jesus multiplied the lad's two small fish and five pieces of bread into enough food to feed the entire crowd, estimated by the gospel of Luke as "about five thousand men" (verse 14).

With their hunger satisfied, the crowd wanted to acclaim Jesus as a "bread Messiah"—a miracle worker who would take care of · their physical needs. But Jesus rejected their attempts and slipped away to a nearby mountain to pray (John 6:14-15). See also *Bread of Life.*

FEEDS FOUR THOUSAND GENTILES. This miracle is similar to Jesus's feeding of the five thousand (see above). In both cases, He multiplied a few pieces of bread and fish to feed many people. But there are also distinct differences between these two events.

The five thousand were a Jewish group in Jewish territory, while the four thousand were a predominantly Gentile crowd in a region known as the Decapolis. Matthew and Mark, in their gospels, included accounts of both events, showing clearly that they considered them two separate miracles (Matthew 14:13-21; 15:29-38; Mark 6:30-44; 8:1-10).

By recording this second feeding miracle, Matthew and Mark may have wanted to show the progressive breaking down of the wall of prejudice through Jesus's ministry. He welcomed all people, regardless of their race or ethnic background. What Jesus did for Jews, He also did for Gentiles. This shows He is the universal Savior. See also *Decapolis*.

F

FESTIVAL OF DEDICATION. See *Feast of Dedication*.

FIELD OF BLOOD. The name given to the plot of ground bought with the money that Judas was paid to betray Jesus. Judas committed suicide on this site. It was also referred to as *akeldama*, an Aramaic term meaning "bloody field" or "field of blood" (Acts 1:18-19).

A slightly different account of this event and the field occurs in Matthew's gospel. Judas wanted to return the betrayal money, but the religious leaders only scoffed. So he threw the thirty silver coins into the temple and went out and hanged himself. Jesus's enemies later used the coins to buy a field where foreigners, or non-Jews, were buried (Matthew 27:3-7).

Visitors to Jerusalem today may visit the reputed site of this field just outside the walls of the Old City. A Greek

Orthodox monastery sits on a hill overlooking the plot. See also *Judas Iscariot.*

FIND ONE'S LIFE BY LOSING IT. Jesus declared, "Whoever finds their life will lose it, and whoever loses their life for my sake will find it" (Matthew 10:39).

With these words, Jesus drew a contrast between the physical life and the spiritual life. People who focus on meeting their own needs may go through life in comfort—or "find" life. But it will eventually become empty and meaningless. By contrast, people who focus on others and doing the will of God—or "losing" their lives—will come to know the true purpose and joy of life.

FIRSTBORN FROM AMONG THE DEAD. A name of Jesus that refers to His victory over death and His promise of eternal life to those who believe in Him. This name comes from the writings of the apostle Paul (Colossians 1:18).

By applying this name to Jesus, Paul did not mean that Jesus was the first person in history to be brought back to life after He had died. In the Old Testament, the prophet Elisha raised the dead son of a widow who had befriended him (2 Kings 4:8–37). And Jesus himself had showed that He was the master over life and death by raising people from the dead on three different occasions (Matthew 9:18–26; Luke 7:11–15; John 11:1–44).

The difference between these resurrections and that of Jesus is that these people eventually died a second time, but He rose from the dead never to die again. As the firstborn from the dead, Jesus guarantees bodily resurrection and eternal life for those who commit their lives to Him.

Paul went on to add that Jesus was the firstborn from among the dead "so that in everything he might have the supremacy" (Colossians 1:18). His universal lordship is a direct result of His resurrection. By overcoming death itself, He has proved there is no power on earth strong enough to hold Him down.

FIRST DAY OF THE WEEK. See *Lord's Day.*

FIRST WILL BE LAST. See *Humble Will Be Exalted.*

FISHING NET. See *Kingdom of God Parables.*

FIVE LOAVES AND TWO FISHES. See *Feeds Five Thousand People.*

FLIGHT INTO EGYPT.

The escape of Joseph and Mary with the child Jesus to avoid the death order of Herod the Great. Joseph was warned in a dream about Herod's plan to kill all male infants in the vicinity of Bethlehem.

Joseph was also told in a dream when it was safe to return to his home in Nazareth after Herod the Great died. This departure from Egypt was a fulfillment of the words of the prophet Hosea: "Out of Egypt I called my son" (Hosea 11:1; see also Matthew 2:15). This prophecy

GOOD NEWS FOR GENTILES

Acts of the Apostles

Decapolis

Demons and Demon Possession, No. 1

Demons and Demon Possession, No. 3

Feeds Four Thousand Gentiles

Galilee

Gentiles

Great Commission

Greeks Ask to See Jesus

Magi

Paul the Apostle

Wedding Banquet Parable

compared the Messiah's leaving Egypt with God's deliverance of His people from slavery in Egypt many centuries before. See also *Slaughter of the Innocents.*

FOOTWASHING. See *Washes the Disciples' Feet.*

FORGIVE THEM, FOR THEY KNOW NOT WHAT THEY DO. See *Seven Sayings from the Cross,* No. 1.

F

FORGIVES WOMAN ACCUSED OF ADULTERY. See *Adultery.*

FRIEND OF TAX COLLECTORS AND SINNERS. See *Associates with Sinners.*

FULFILLMENT OF THE LAW. In His Sermon on the Mount, Jesus told His disciples that He had come not to abolish the law but to fulfill it (Matthew 5:17-18). He probably meant that His teachings filled the Old Testament law with meaning that had never been emphasized before. For example, the law stated, "Do not murder." But Jesus declared, "Do not even hate" (see Matthew 5:21-22). So He fulfilled the law by going beyond its outward requirements to the inner spiritual principles on which it was based.

Early New Testament writers picked up on this theme. Both James, the half brother of Jesus, and Paul the apostle emphasized that love is the fulfillment of the law (James 2:8; Romans 13:8-10; Galatians 5:14).

FULLNESS OF TIME. A concept, stated by the apostle Paul, that God sent Jesus at exactly the right time in world history (Galatians 4:4). The old Greek and Roman gods had lost their appeal, and people were longing for something more personal; even Judaism had degenerated into a meaningless system of rituals and law-keeping. Jesus Christ offered a new and refreshing belief system that brought meaning and purpose to those who placed their faith in Him.

God's timing in sending Jesus was also perfect because of the peaceful conditions that existed throughout the Mediterranean world. This *Pax Romana* was accomplished by the ruling Romans, who had also built good roads throughout the region. In addition, Greek was the dominant language of the region. All these conditions contributed to the rapid spread of the gospel in the years after Jesus's resurrection and ascension.

GABBATHA. See *Stone Pavement.*

GABRIEL. An angel who announced to the virgin Mary that she would give birth to Jesus, the long-awaited Savior and Messiah (Luke 1:26-37). Just a few months before, Gabriel had also foretold the birth of Jesus's forerunner, John the Baptist (Luke 1:8-20). Centuries before, in Old Testament times, Gabriel had also appeared to the prophet Daniel (Daniel 8:15-16).

This message to Mary is memorialized today at the Greek Orthodox Church of St. Gabriel, also known as the Church of the Annunciation. The building sits over an underground spring, which is said to be the site where Mary was drawing water when Gabriel made his startling appearance. See also *Annunciation of Jesus's Birth.*

GADARA. See *Decapolis.*

GALILEE. A Roman province in northern Israel during New Testament times and the district where Jesus spent about two years during His early ministry. Using the town of Capernaum on the shore of the Sea of Galilee as a base, Jesus and His disciples traveled throughout the surrounding province of Galilee to teach and heal (Mark 1:38-39).

This province was known as "Galilee of the nations" (Isaiah 9:1), or "Galilee of the Gentiles" (Matthew 4:15) because of the influence of several surrounding Gentile territories.

Jesus grew up in Nazareth, a Galilean village. All of His disciples were natives of this province except for the betrayer Judas Iscariot. The name *Iscariot* seems to derive from the town of Kerioth in the province of Judea, south of Galilee (Luke 22:3). See also *Sea of Galilee*.

GATE FOR THE SHEEP. See *Good Shepherd*.

GENEALOGIES OF JESUS. Since Jesus had no human father and was born through miraculous conception, some people claim it's not possible to trace His human ancestry. On the other hand, He was fully human, emerging from the womb of Mary through the natural biological process that brings babies into the world.

This, in a nutshell, is the dilemma presented by the family trees of Jesus recorded in the gospels of Matthew (1:1-17) and Luke (3:23-38). Though divinely conceived and existing before time began, He was also born from a woman's womb into the world at a specific point in time.

Everyone agrees that these two genealogies do not list exactly the same people in the same order, although some people such as David and the patriarchs do appear in both accounts. Both gospel writers included only selected names—perhaps because they supported the purpose Matthew and Luke had in mind when they wrote their respective accounts.

Matthew, for example, traced Jesus's human family line back to Abraham, the father of the Jewish nation (Matthew 1:2). Matthew wanted to show that Jesus was the fulfillment of God's promise to Abraham—namely, to build a godly nation that would serve as His witnesses to the rest of the world (Genesis 12:1–3). This promise was fulfilled in a spiritual sense through the life and ministry of Jesus.

Luke traced Jesus's human ancestry all the way back to Adam, the first man (Luke 3:38). Since Luke wrote his gospel for Gentiles, the purpose of his genealogy was to emphasize the universal nature of Jesus's mission. As the Last Adam, Jesus solved the sin problem created by the first Adam's disobedience to the Lord.

GENNESARET. See *Sea of Galilee.*

GENTILES. Non-Jews, or people of any nationality

JESUS AND PRAYER

Ask, and You Will Receive

Demons and Demon Possession, No. 2

Eye for Eye

Gethsemane

High Priestly Prayer of Jesus

Lord's Prayer

Mount of Olives

Persistent Widow Parable

Prayer

Proud Pharisee Parable

Remain in Me

Sermon on the Mount, No. 6

other than the Jewish race. Jews considered Gentiles as unworthy of God's love. Jesus rejected this notion and made several trips into Gentile territory to teach and heal (Matthew 15:21; Mark 7:31).

In His final charge to His followers, Jesus also made it clear that they were to present the gospel to people of all nations (Matthew 28:16-20). See also *Acts of the Apostles*; *Demons and Demon Possession*, No. 3; *Feeds Four Thousand Gentiles*.

GERASA. See *Decapolis*.

GETHSEMANE. A garden on or near the Mount of Olives where Jesus, facing the reality of His approaching death, struggled to fulfill God's will. The human side of His nature wanted to avoid the cross, but He knew this was His destiny—part of God's plan for the redemption of humankind. Jesus conquered this temptation and fear, resolving to follow the will of His heavenly Father (Mark 14:32-42).

With Jesus in the garden were His three closest disciples—Peter, James, and John. He told them to stand watch while He went off alone to pray. At the Last Supper just a few hours before, these three—along with the other disciples—had insisted that they would never betray Jesus (Mark 14:31). Now, tired from the activities of a busy day, they failed to stay awake for even one hour to support their friend in His hour of desperate need.

The garden of Gethsemane today is one of the most popular sites visited by Holy Land pilgrims. Filled with ancient olive trees, it occupies part of the outer courtyard of the Church of All Nations, also known as the Church of the Agony. This church was built with contributions from people throughout the world. See also *Mount of Olives*.

GOD-MAN. See *Humanity of Jesus*.

GOLD, FRANKINCENSE, AND MYRRH. See *Magi*.

GOLDEN RULE. A familiar saying of Jesus, from His Sermon on the Mount, that believers should treat others as they would like to be treated (Matthew 7:12). Some critics claim that this principle is not unique to the teachings of Jesus, and it's true that the Jewish rabbi Hillel said about a century before Jesus's time, "Do not do to thy neighbor what is hateful to thyself." Other great teachers of history—such as Socrates and Confucius—have made statements similar to Hillel's.

But notice that this rabbi's saying is negative and passive rather than positive and active in nature. By contrast, Jesus taught His followers to take the initiative in showing kindness to others. Christianity is more than avoiding sin in our lives; it is practicing positive goodness toward other people—going out of our way to show His love for them in practical ways.

Jesus enlarged on His Golden Rule with these words: "For this sums up the Law and the Prophets." In other words, all the declarations of the Old Testament law and the moral teachings of Israel's great prophets may be summed up in these eleven simple words: "Do to others what you would have them do to you."

GOLGOTHA. See *Skull, The*.

GOOD SAMARITAN PARABLE. This well-known parable grew out of Jesus's discussion about love and compassion with an expert in the law (Luke 10:25-37). This man agreed that loving one's neighbor was an important teaching of the Old Testament law (Leviticus 19:18). But he asked Jesus, "Who is my neighbor?" Perhaps this man was seeking the truth, but he may have been trying to trick Jesus into making an inappropriate response.

Jesus told this expert in the law about a Jewish man who was traveling from Jerusalem to Jericho. On this perilous road, thieves robbed and beat the man—even taking his clothes—and left him by the side of the road to die. Two Jewish religious leaders, a priest and a Levite, came by and saw the helpless man. But they ignored him and continued on their journey. Perhaps they were in a hurry to get to their next religious appointment.

But a kind Samaritan happened by and took pity on the wounded traveler. The Samaritan treated the man's wounds and even took him to a nearby inn. There, he directed the innkeeper to take care of the man and even paid for the man's lodging while he recuperated.

Jesus knew that Jews hated Samaritans, who were considered half-breeds. Yet He deliberately made a member of this despised race the hero of this parable. Now it was Jesus's turn to ask a question: "Which of these three do you think was a neighbor to the man who fell into the hands of robbers?" (verse 36).

This Jewish official had to admit that the kind Samaritan was the one who showed a neighborly attitude toward this unfortunate traveler. The message of the parable was unmistakably clear: true neighbors are those who show love and compassion to people in need. See also *Samaria*.

GOOD SHEPHERD. A name of Jesus that pictures Him as a compassionate guide who loves and protects His people, just as a shepherd cares for the sheep in his flock. Jesus applied this imagery to himself in a long dialogue with the Pharisees, recorded in the gospel of John (10:1-18).

A shepherd caring for a flock of sheep was a familiar scene in New Testament times. The people knew all about a heroic lad named David, who protected his father's sheep by fending off wild animals that attacked the flock (1 Samuel 17:34-36). The Jews were also familiar with the Twenty-Third Psalm and its imagery of the Lord as a shepherd of His people.

Jesus used this familiar imagery to contrast himself with the Pharisees and other religious leaders. They claimed to be leaders of God's people, but they were actually false prophets who were leading them astray.

Jesus described himself as "the gate for the sheep" (verse 7; *door of the sheep:* KJV). When a flock of sheep was bedded down in an enclosed area for the night, the shepherd slept at the entrance to keep the sheep in and predators out. Jesus was willing to lay His life on the line—all the way to the cross—to protect and save His people.

A shepherd knew his sheep, and had a special call for them. They recognized their shepherd's voice and commands. He would call them to pastures and pools of water where they could graze and drink. Like a good shepherd, Jesus is a leader—not a driver—of His sheep. His believers follow Him because they know He wants only the best for His flock.

Another name of Jesus that uses this imagery of a shepherd is "Overseer of your souls." The apostle Peter reminded the readers of his epistle what their lives had been like before they put their faith in the Savior. "'You were like sheep going astray,'" he told them, "but now you have returned to the Shepherd and Overseer of your souls" (1 Peter 2:25).

G

GORDON'S CALVARY. See *Skull, The.*

GOSPEL. The good news of the coming of the kingdom of God in the person of Jesus and the deliverance from sin that He offers humankind (Matthew 9:35; Acts 14:7).

GOSPELS. The four books at the beginning of the New Testament—Matthew, Mark, Luke, and John—that tell us about the life and ministry of Jesus.

These gospels are not exactly biographies, since they focus mainly on the last three years of His life. They tell us nothing about Jesus's growing-up years, with the exception of His discussion with learned teachers in Jerusalem when He was twelve (Luke 2:41-49).

The writers of Matthew, Mark, Luke, and John recorded only what they considered the most important events from Jesus's three-year ministry. The apostle John admitted this at the end of his gospel: "Jesus did many other things as well. If every one of them were written down, I suppose that even the whole world would not have room for the books that would be written" (John 21:25).

The main purpose of the gospel writers was to show how God revealed himself in a unique way through the work of His Son. Each writer did so from a different perspective and with a unique audience in mind. All four gospels are essential for a complete understanding of Jesus and His message. See also *John, Gospel of; Luke, Gospel of; Mark, Gospel of; Matthew, Gospel of; Synoptic Gospels.*

GREAT BANQUET PARABLE. Jesus told about the master of a household, apparently a man of means, who invited all his friends to an elaborate banquet. All he asked of them was to show up and enjoy the meal (Luke 14:15-24). But the man's generous invitation was met with nothing but weak excuses. One by one, the guests explained they could not come because they had other things to do.

Angered by these refusals, the master instructed his servant to invite the poor and disabled throughout the city to come and enjoy the meal. These were the "street people" of Jesus's time. What the upper crust of society had turned down, members of the lower class were allowed to enjoy.

Some of Jesus's more astute listeners may have recognized that He was referring in this parable to the Jewish nation. God had planned a "grand banquet"—an opportunity for fellowship between himself and the Jews, His chosen people. But they continually rejected His invitation by falling into sin and rebelling against His commandments.

Now the Lord, through the person of His Son, Jesus, had opened the way for Gentiles to experience His love and fellowship. The Jews, because of their rejection of Jesus, were turning down God's gracious invitation. But the pagan Gentiles, considered outcasts by the Jewish people, were coming into God's kingdom because of their openness to the teachings of Jesus.

Another parable of Jesus, recorded in Matthew's gospel (22:1–10), drives home the same point. See also *Wedding Banquet Parable*.

GREAT COMMISSION. Jesus's directive to His followers to continue His mission in the world by presenting the gospel to people both near and far. This command to make disciples and baptize and teach them has been called the "marching orders" of the church. It applies to believers of every generation (Matthew 28:19–20).

While the wording of Matthew's gospel is the most familiar, the commission appears in abbreviated form in the other two Synoptic Gospels as well as the book of Acts (Mark 16:15; Luke 24:47–48; Acts 1:8).

Carrying out Jesus's orders is not easy, but offers great rewards for believers who take the duty seriously. Christians will often be criticized and ridiculed when they present the gospel to unbelievers, but this is offset by the joy they feel at the positive response of those who turn to Christ. He has promised to give strength to obey His command: "Surely I am with you always," He declared, "to the very end of the age" (Matthew 28:20). See also *Acts of the Apostles; Keys of the Kingdom of Heaven.*

GREATEST COMMANDMENT. A Pharisee once asked Jesus His opinion on which commandment in the law of Moses was the greatest of all. This was probably a trick question. No matter how

Jesus answered, He was certain to leave out some commandment that His enemies considered more important (Matthew 22:34-40).

Jesus responded by quoting an Old Testament verse known as the *shema*—the injunction to love God with one's total being (Deuteronomy 6:5)—as the greatest commandment. But He went on to cite another that is just as important: the directive to love one's neighbor as oneself (Leviticus 19:18).

Jesus was saying that our claim to love God is a sham unless it causes us to love others—to treat them with respect and compassion.

GREED. *See Possessions.*

GREEKS ASK TO SEE JESUS. During the Passover celebration in Jerusalem just before Jesus was crucified, a group of Greeks requested an audience with Him. These Gentiles were probably attracted to the ethical teachings of Judaism; they wanted to learn more from this miracle-working Jewish teacher of whom they had heard (John 12:20-36).

Their request moved Jesus deeply. In these foreigners who were seeking the truth, He envisioned a future ingathering of people of all nationalities who would respond to the gospel. At the same time, He realized the time for His sacrificial death was drawing near.

For a fleeting moment Jesus considered asking God the Father to deliver Him from what He knew would be a painful death, just as He would pray a short time later in the garden of Gethsemane. But then He turned away from that temptation with the determination to pursue the path that led to the cross. Only in this way could He achieve the mission for which His heavenly Father had sent Him into the world. He prayed that His atoning sacrifice would bring glory to God's name.

In an audible voice from heaven, God responded, "I have glorified it, and will glorify it again" (John 12:28). This voice had spoken twice before—at Jesus's baptism (Matthew 3:17) and at His transfiguration (Luke 9:35). Now Jesus was assured that this divine presence would be with Him all the way to the cross. See also *Gentiles*.

HEAD OF THE CHURCH.

A title of Jesus that underscores His role as founder and sustainer of the community of believers who are devoted to Him and His teachings. This title comes from the teachings of the apostle Paul (Ephesians 5:23).

Jesus knew from the very beginning that His time on earth was limited, so He selected twelve disciples who would spend time with Him and learn from His teachings. These followers were slow to learn exactly who Jesus was and the purpose of His mission as the Son of God. But they eventually caught on and adopted His mission as their own. Eventually, these disciples became known as *apostles*, Jesus's earthly representatives who passed on to others what they had seen and heard. Their testimony

JESUS'S ASSOCIATION WITH WOMEN

Adultery

Anointing of Jesus

Demons and Demon Possession, No. 3

Demons and Demon Possession, No. 7

Demons and Demon Possession, No. 8

Jacob's Well

Jairus's Daughter Raised from the Dead

Joanna

Luke, Gospel of

Martha

Mary Magdalene

Mary, Sister of Lazarus

Nain

Salome

Susanna

Widow's Sacrificial Offering

Widow's Son Raised from the Dead

Woman at the Well

Woman with Hemorrhage Healed

Women at the Cross and Tomb

formed the bedrock of the church, a body of believers—now worldwide in scope—whose purpose is to continue Jesus's work of redemption in the world.

Jesus is the head of the church, and we as believers make up the body (1 Corinthians 12:27). Obviously, Christ as the head of the church is no longer physically present on earth—so the members of His body, the church, are His earthly representatives. To them falls the responsibility of continuing His work in the world. See also *Great Commission; Keys of the Kingdom of Heaven.*

HEALINGS OF JESUS. See *Miracles of Jesus.*

HELL. See *Rich Man and Lazarus Parable.*

HERMON. See *Mount Hermon.*

HEROD. A dynasty of Roman rulers in the time of Jesus. Four different Herods are mentioned in the Gospels.

1. **Herod the Great.** This Herod ruled over Palestine when Jesus was born. He ordered the slaughter of innocent infants in Bethlehem when he learned that a new king (Jesus) had been born there. Joseph took Mary and the child Jesus to Egypt to escape this death threat (Matthew 2:13-15). When Herod died, three of his sons took over parts of the territory he had ruled.

2. **Herod Archelaus.** This son of Herod the Great became ruler over Judea in southern Palestine. When Joseph, Mary, and Jesus returned from Egypt, they passed through Archelaus's territory on their way to Galilee (Matthew 2:22).

3. **Herod Antipas.** This Herod inherited the territories of Galilee in northern Palestine and Perea east of the Jordan River.

He ordered the execution of John the Baptist (Mark 6:17-29). But Antipas refused to pass judgment on Jesus when He appeared before Pilate in Jerusalem (Luke 23:6-12).

4. **Herod Philip.** This son of Herod the Great became ruler in extreme northern Galilee. Philip was in power when Jesus began His public ministry (Luke 3:1).

HERODIANS. A group of prosperous and influential Jews who supported the rule of the Roman government over their homeland. They joined forces with the Pharisees against Jesus, perhaps because they feared His teachings and actions would bring reprisals from Rome and threaten their privileged position (Mark 3:6).

This fear was particularly apparent when the Herodians and Pharisees together asked Jesus if it was appropriate for the Jewish nation to pay taxes to their Roman overlords. The two groups were hoping to create trouble for Jesus by whatever answer He gave. If He said yes, they figured, the people would be offended; if He said no, Roman officials would see Him as a troublemaker (Matthew 22:15-22). But Jesus avoided their trap with a clever answer: "Give back to Caesar what is Caesar's," He replied, "and to God what is God's" (verse 21).

By this answer, Jesus established the principle that the secular state or nation has a right to take material support from its subjects, but only God has jurisdiction in matters of the human soul. See also *Roman Empire*.

HIDDEN TREASURE. See *Kingdom of God Parables*.

HIGH PRIEST. The highest ranking of all the priests over the Jewish people. He served as administrator and supervisor of the entire priestly system.

The high priesthood was established in Old Testament times with the appointment of Moses's brother, Aaron, to this position (Exodus 28:1–29:46). For many centuries the office was hereditary, with the oldest son of the high priest succeeding his father in this responsibility. But in New Testament times, the ruling Roman government appointed and deposed high priests at will. This led the high priesthood to degenerate into a political rather than a religious office.

During New Testament era, the high priest presided over deliberations of the Sanhedrin, the Jewish high court. The high priest Caiaphas presided at the Jewish trial of Jesus and declared Him guilty of blasphemy (Matthew 26:57–65).

The writer of the book of Hebrews referred to Jesus as the "great high priest" (Hebrews 4:14). He is superior to the high priest, who repeatedly offered sacrificial animals on the altar to deal with the sins of the people of Israel. By contrast, Jesus gave His own life on the cross as the once-for-all sacrifice for the sins of the entire world. See also *Caiaphas*; *Sanhedrin*.

H

HIGH PRIESTLY PRAYER OF JESUS. The longest recorded prayer of Jesus during His earthly ministry, covering an entire chapter in John's gospel (John 17). It is called the high priestly prayer because Jesus took on the role of the high priest of Israel in making intercession for His people.

Jesus first recognized that the time for the accomplishment of His redemptive mission was fast approaching. He prayed that God would fill Him with the Father's glory and that He in turn would glorify God through His sacrificial death (verses 1–5).

Next Jesus prayed for His disciples whom He had taught patiently for more than three years. He prayed that they would remain faithful to these divine truths and that God would protect them from Satan as they continued His work in the world (verses 6–19).

In the third section of the prayer, Jesus interceded for all people of the future who would place their faith in Him. He wanted them to be unified in a common purpose—to become a host of witnesses who would demonstrate to the world the love and moral character of their Savior (verses 20-26). When believers read this part of the prayer today, they should be energized by the reality that Jesus prayed for them two thousand years ago. See also *Lord's Prayer.*

HOLY SPIRIT. As Jesus looked toward His death, resurrection, and ascension, He promised His disciples that He would continue to abide with them through His living presence as the Holy Spirit.

Jesus described the Spirit as "another Counselor" (John 14:16 HCSB). The word *another* in this context means "another of the same kind." The word *Counselor* expresses the idea of someone called alongside to offer assistance and guidance. Thus, the Counselor would be someone like Jesus himself—a living presence who would give the disciples the same kind of help that Jesus had provided while He was with them in body.

Another phrase that Jesus used for the Holy Spirit was "the Spirit of truth" (John 15:26). The Holy Spirit represented the One who was "the way and the truth and the life" (John 14:6). Jesus was assuring His disciples that if they followed the leadership of the Spirit, they would always walk in the truth.

Jesus's promise to strengthen His disciples with the Holy Spirit was dramatically realized soon after His ascension into heaven. While the believers celebrated the feast of Pentecost in Jerusalem, they were filled with the Holy Spirit as He came in the appearance of a flame to rest on each of them (Acts 2:1-3). This outpouring of God's Spirit led to a great sermon by the apostle Peter (Acts 2:14-40) and the conversion of three thousand people (Acts 2:41).

HOLY WEEK. The final week of Jesus's earthly life that ended with His death and His resurrection from the dead. It is also known as Passion Week, with the word *passion* referring to His suffering.

Each of the gospel writers devotes several chapters to this week, although it was a small part of His ministry of about three years. They considered the events of these seven days the crowning achievement of Jesus's mission as the Messiah. Here's a brief summary of the main events of this significant week in His life and ministry, as reported in the four gospels:

Sunday (Palm Sunday). Jesus makes His triumphal entry into Jerusalem (Matthew 21:1–9).

Monday. Jesus clears the temple of money exchangers and merchants (Mark 11:11–19) and curses a fig tree (Mark 11:12, 20).

Tuesday. Jesus predicts the destruction of Jerusalem and His future return (Matthew 24:3–25); Mary of Bethany anoints Him with expensive perfume (John 12:3); Judas plots with the Jewish religious leaders to betray Jesus into their hands (Matthew 26:14–15).

Thursday Evening (Maundy Thursday). Jesus observes the Jewish Passover by eating a ceremonial meal with His disciples (Luke 22:7–12); He turns this meal into a memorial of His death known as the Lord's Supper (Luke 22:17–20); He washes His disciples' feet in a gesture of humble service (John 13:1–5); He agonizes in prayer in the garden of Gethsemane for God's will to be done (Matthew 26:36–42).

Friday (Good Friday). Jesus is betrayed by Judas and arrested by enemies (Luke 22:47–48); He undergoes a trial for blasphemy before the Jewish Sanhedrin (Mark 14:53–65); Peter denies three times that he knows Jesus (Luke 22:54–62); He appears before Pilate, the Roman governor, who sentences Him to death by crucifixion (Mark 15:1–15); Joseph of Arimathea claims the body of Jesus and buries it in his own new tomb (John 19:38–42).

Sunday (Easter Sunday). Jesus is resurrected from the dead (Mark 16:1–6); He appears to Mary Magdalene at the tomb early in the morning (John 20:10–18) and to His disciples later that day (John 20:19–23).

HOSANNA. See *Triumphal Entry into Jerusalem.*

HOUSEHOLDER. See *Owner of a House Parable.*

HOUSE BUILT ON A ROCK. See *Sermon on the Mount,* No. 10.

HUMANITY OF JESUS. The doctrine that Jesus was fully human and existed in a physical body as a man, although He was also the divine Son of God. He is often referred to as the God-man, a title that refers to this dual nature.

Most believers tend to emphasize Jesus's divinity more than His humanity. But the clear teaching of the New Testament is that His human side was an essential part of His nature (John 1:14; 1 Timothy 3:16). Throughout Christian history, various theories have been proposed to undermine the humanity of Jesus, but the church has always rejected these false teachings. The Nicene Creed, approved by leaders at the Council of Nicea in AD 325, declared, "He became flesh by the Holy Spirit of the virgin Mary and was made man."

For evidence of Jesus's full identification with humankind, we need look no farther than Mark's gospel. Mark portrays His human side more graphically than any other New Testament writer. Jesus grew tired (4:38) and was moved to anger (11:15-17). He was not above being displeased (10:14), amazed (6:6), and disappointed (8:12). He also experienced sorrow and distress like any other person (14:34).

The writer of the New Testament book of Hebrews described Jesus as our great high priest who could sympathize with us in our weakness. Then he added these comforting words: "We have one who has been tempted in every way, just as we are—yet he did not sin. Let us then approach God's throne of grace with confidence, so that we may receive mercy and find grace to help us in our time of need" (Hebrews 4:15–16). See also *Incarnation of Jesus; Temptations of Jesus.*

HUMBLE WILL BE EXALTED. A phrase from Jesus's pronunciation of woe against the Pharisees (Matthew 23:12). They considered themselves superior to the common people and loved to be praised and recognized by the crowds.

In contrast to the Pharisees' pompous pride, Jesus declared that true greatness consists of lowering oneself to the position of a servant. Those who do so will be recognized and rewarded by the Lord. Jesus also declared on one occasion, "Many who are first shall be last; and the last shall be first" (Matthew 19:30 KJV). God's standard of judgment is rooted in divine truth rather than the false values of a fickle world. See also *Woes against the Pharisees.*

HYPOCRISY. See *Pharisees; Woes against the Pharisees.*

"I AM" STATEMENTS OF JESUS. Seven metaphors in the gospel of John that Jesus used as a form of self-identification. Through these figures of speech, He declared who He was, why He had been sent into the world, and what He provides for those who become His followers.

1. **"I am the bread of life"** (John 6:35). Jesus offers spiritual sustenance to believers. Those who place their faith in Him will have their hunger for God and His righteousness forever satisfied. See *Bread of Life.*

2. **"I am the light of the world"** (John 8:12). Jesus offers guidance and direction to a world hopelessly lost in darkness. Apart from Him, we have no hope for deliverance from the bondage of sin. See *Light of the World.*

3. **"I am the gate for the sheep"** (John 10:7). Jesus cares for and protects those who belong to Him. Salvation is found in

none other than Him; He is the entry point into righteousness and eternal life. See *Good Shepherd*.

4. **"I am the good shepherd"** (John 10:11, 14). Jesus protects His people, keeping close watch over them. Those who believe in Him are safe and secure under His watchful eye. See *Good Shepherd*.

5. **"I am the resurrection and the life"** (John 11:25). Jesus is the Lord of life and the victor over death. The grave will not have the last word for believers. They will live on in the afterlife in eternal fellowship with Him.

6. **"I am the way and the truth and the life"** (John 14:6). As the source of all truth about God, Jesus is the only way to the Father. Those who believe in Him find a reason for being, as well as the promise of eternal life when this life on earth comes to an end.

7. **"I am the true vine"** (John 15:1). Believers are like branches that grow from the main vine. Jesus's love flows through us as we bear fruit for the good of the kingdom of God. See *True Vine*.

IDUMEA. Greek name for the region known as Edom in Old Testament times. This territory was near the Dead Sea in southern Judea. Crowds from Idumea heard about Jesus's miracles and traveled to Galilee to see Him early in His ministry (Mark 3:8).

IMMANUEL. A title of Jesus that emphasizes God's eternal presence with His people through the person of His Son. The word is a Hebrew term that means "God with us."

According to the gospel of Matthew, Jesus's birth was the fulfillment of a prophecy by the prophet Isaiah several centuries before Jesus was born (Matthew 1:22–23; Isaiah 7:14; *Emmanuel*: KJV). Jesus came to earth in the form of a man to show that God is for humankind in its hopeless and sinful condition.

This declaration of God's presence occurs again as the very last verse of Matthew's gospel. Before His ascension back to His Father in heaven, Jesus assured His followers, "Surely I am with you always, to the very end of the age" (Matthew 28:20).

JESUS'S ATTITUDE TOWARD "SINNERS"

IMPURE SPIRITS. See *Demons and Demon Possession.*

INCARNATION OF JESUS. The doctrine that Jesus took on human flesh in order to identify with fallen humankind and to save people from their sins. The word *incarnate* means "embodied in flesh." Jesus was the divine Son of God clothed in a physical body. He can sympathize with us in all the experiences, feelings, joys, and sorrows that are common to the human race (Hebrews 4:15). See also *Humanity of Jesus.*

ISAIAH. A famous Old Testament prophet who foretold the coming of the Messiah (Isaiah 7:14). Jesus identified himself as the Suffering Servant whom Isaiah had written about. This divine agent of the Lord was rejected by His own people, but became the agent of redemption for all people (Isaiah 61:1–3; Luke 4:16–21; *Esaias:* KJV).

Jesus claimed to be this Suffering Servant when he read from Isaiah's writings in the synagogue at Nazareth, His hometown. At His claim that this servant of the Lord would extend God's redemption to the Gentiles, the people exploded in anger and tried to throw Him off a cliff at the edge of town. But Jesus miraculously escaped and returned to Capernaum to continue His ministry in the district of Galilee (Luke 4:28-30). See also *Messianic Prophecies.*

ISCARIOT. See *Judas Iscariot.*

IT IS FINISHED. See *Seven Sayings from the Cross,* No. 6.

JACOB. See *Star Out of Jacob.*

JACOB'S WELL. An ancient water source where Jesus talked with a sinful Samaritan woman and offered her the water of life (John 4:4-26). The well is named for the patriarch Jacob, who may have dug it many centuries before Jesus's time. After returning to Canaan from his uncle Laban's home in Mesopotamia, Jacob lived in the area where the well was located (Genesis 33:16-20).

A deep well still stands on the site today. It is probably the very water source from which Jesus asked this woman to give Him a drink. The well sits within the complex of the Bir Ya'qub Monastery owned by the Eastern Orthodox Church. Thousands of Holy Land tourists visit the site every year. See also *Woman at the Well.*

JAIRUS'S DAUGHTER RAISED FROM THE DEAD. Jairus was a leader in the synagogue at Capernaum, Jesus's headquarters in the region of Galilee. This man fell at Jesus's feet and begged Him to heal his daughter, who was critically ill (Mark 5:21–43).

Jesus began to follow Jairus to his house. But He was interrupted by a woman with a hemorrhage who wanted to be healed. It must have been agonizing for Jairus, with his own little daughter at the point of death, to stand aside as Jesus dealt with this woman. During the delay, messengers arrived with the devastating news that the girl had died.

Jesus ignored their words and continued His journey toward Jairus's house. When He arrived, He heard the familiar sound of mourners, wailing for the dead girl. Jesus dismissed them, took the girl by the hand, and directed her in the Aramaic language, *"Talitha koum!"* ("Little girl, I say to you, get up," verse 41). These were the words a loving parent would say when arousing a child from sleep. Immediately the girl got up and began to walk.

All the people in the house were astonished at this miracle. But Jesus asked them not to tell anyone what they had seen. He was concerned that the crowds would think of Him as just a worker of miracles and wonders, not the spiritual deliverer He came to be.

JAMES, BROTHER OF JOHN. A son of Zebedee who left his trade as a fisherman on the Sea of Galilee to become a disciple of Jesus (Matthew 4:21-23). He is often referred to as James the Great or James the Elder to distinguish him from another James among Jesus's disciples—James, the son of Alphaeus.

James and his brother John were known for their quick tempers. On one occasion they urged Jesus to destroy a Samaritan village for rejecting Jesus and the disciples (Luke 9:51-56). James was also ambitious: he joined his brother to ask Jesus to give them places of honor in His coming kingdom (Mark 10:35-40).

In spite of these human flaws, James became a stalwart witness for Jesus in the early days of the church, and he was the first disciple to suffer martyrdom for his faith. The Roman ruler Herod Agrippa I had James put to death in his campaign to suppress the church and win the favor of his Jewish subjects (Acts 12:1–3). See also *Disciples of Jesus.*

JAMES, HALF BROTHER OF JESUS. A brother of Jesus born by natural means after Jesus's supernatural conception in Mary's womb. At first skeptical of Jesus and His work, James eventually became a believer and rose to a position of leadership in the early church in Jerusalem (Galatians 2:1–10). He was probably the author of the epistle of James in the New Testament.

James apparently presided at a meeting of church leaders in Jerusalem to deal with the issue of Gentile conversions. Some leaders thought these non-Jewish converts had to be circumcised before they could be saved (Acts 15:1–21). But James issued the group's decision that "we should not make it difficult for the Gentiles who are turning to God" (verse 19), and that Jewish rituals were not necessary for salvation.

In attendance at this meeting was the apostle Paul. This decision paved the way for the explosive growth of the church under his later ministry as the apostle to the Gentiles. See also *Brothers of Jesus.*

JAMES, SON OF ALPHAEUS. A disciple of Jesus also referred to as James the younger (Mark 15:40). He appears in the lists of Jesus's disciples, but is never mentioned again. See also *Disciples of Jesus.*

JEREMIAH. An Old Testament prophet known for his prophecy of a new covenant that would replace the old covenant between God and His people (Jeremiah 31:31-34). This prediction was fulfilled through the life and death of Jesus Christ.

When Jesus ate the Passover meal with His disciples, he referred to what they ate and drank together as "the new covenant in my blood, which is poured out for you" (Luke 22:20). The author of the book of Hebrews picked up on this imagery by describing Jesus as "the mediator of a new covenant" (Hebrews 12:24).

This new covenant was inaugurated by the death of Jesus on the cross. His sacrifice replaces the old covenant that God made with His people in Old Testament times, atoning for sin and restoring the relationship between God and those individuals who place their faith in Him.

JERICHO. A city about twelve miles northeast of Jerusalem where Jesus healed a blind beggar known as Bartimaeus (Mark 10:46-52) and encountered Zacchaeus, a dishonest tax collector (Luke 19:1-10). Jericho was also the setting for Jesus's famous parable about the good Samaritan, a kind man who stopped to help a stranger who'd been robbed, beaten, and left for dead (Luke 10:25-37).

This city of Jesus's time is known as New Testament Jericho. It grew up about two miles from the site of Old Testament Jericho, which was destroyed by Joshua during his conquest of Canaan and never rebuilt (Joshua 6:1-26).

A high hill known as the Mount of Temptation may be seen from the ruins of Old Testament Jericho. This is reputed to be the site where Satan tempted Jesus at the beginning of His public ministry (Luke 4:1-13).

JERUSALEM. The Jewish religious and political capital where Jesus was resurrected after being arrested and crucified by His enemies. This major population center of Israel is often referred to as the Holy City.

But Jesus, the Holy One, met a cool reception in the Holy City. Its religious leaders resented His miraculous works, His rejection of their human traditions, and His refusal to bow down to their authority. Jesus expressed great sorrow over Jerusalem because of its sin and indifference and the refusal of its religious officials to accept Him as the Messiah (Matthew 23:37-39).

Jesus rode triumphantly into the city and cleared the temple of merchants and moneychangers (Matthew 21:12-13). This was a direct challenge to the religious establishment and an affirmation of His God-given authority.

Forty days after His resurrection in Jerusalem, from a site not far from the city, Jesus was taken up into heaven (Acts 1:6-12). Jerusalem is also where the early church got its start, as the Holy Spirit empowered early believers who were in the city to celebrate the Pentecost festival (Acts 2:1-12). After this miraculous outpouring, the apostle Peter delivered a powerful sermon that resulted in the addition of three thousand believers to the church (Acts 2:40-41). See also *Laments over Jerusalem.*

J

JOANNA. One of several women who followed Jesus and provided food for Him and His disciples. Luke's gospel identifies her as the wife of Chuza, who was the manager of Herod Antipas's household (Luke 8:1-3).

This is probably the same Joanna who went to the tomb on resurrection morning with several other women to anoint Jesus's body with spices. Two angels told the women that Jesus had been resurrected, and they reported this good news to the disciples (Luke 24:1-11). See also *Women at the Cross and Tomb.*

JOHN THE APOSTLE. A disciple of Jesus who wrote the gospel of John. He is sometimes called "the beloved disciple" since he identified himself as "the disciple whom Jesus loved" (John 21:7). As He hung on the cross, Jesus directed John to take care of His mother, Mary (19:26–27).

John was part of the trio often referred to as the "inner circle" of Jesus's disciples. Along with the other two members of this group—his brother James and the apostle Peter—John was with Jesus at His transfiguration (Matthew 17:1–6), His prayer in the garden of Gethsemane (Mark 14:32–42), and the raising of Jairus's daughter from the dead (Mark 5:37–43).

Informed of the empty tomb on Easter morning, John outran Peter to the site and looked inside. In his gospel, John records of himself that he "saw and believed" (John 20:8). Though all the disciples were slow to understand that Jesus had risen from the dead, John was perhaps the first to grasp that reality.

After Jesus's ascension, John worked with the apostle Peter to witness boldly for Jesus in the city of Jerusalem (Acts 4:1–5).

John may have been one of the youngest members of the Twelve. Many believe he was the last of the disciples to die, after writing the epistles of first, second, and third John and the book of Revelation. See also *Disciples of Jesus*.

J

JOHN THE BAPTIST. The bold prophet who baptized Jesus at the beginning of His public ministry and otherwise prepared the way for His inauguration of the kingdom of God. John's mother, Elizabeth, and Jesus's mother, Mary, were relatives (Luke 1:36), so the two men probably knew each other as distant kinsmen.

John lived in the wilderness, where he foraged for food— surviving on wild honey and locusts. He wore clothes made from the hair and skin of animals. Through these actions, he identified with the prophets of Israel's past such as Elijah, men who were called to speak for the Lord.

Many people were drawn to John's distinctive lifestyle and pattern of preaching. He called on them to repent and get ready for the arrival of Jesus (Luke 3:1-18), whom he identified as his superior. When Jesus arrived on the scene, John identified Him as the Lamb of God whose atoning sacrifice would save people from their sin (John 1:29).

John's ministry continued after Jesus began to teach and heal. One of John's own followers, Andrew, eventually became a disciple of Jesus (John 1:35-42). But John never complained about this or the larger crowds that followed Jesus—he believed it was God's plan for Jesus to take front and center while John faded into the background (John 3:26-30).

John's bold preaching eventually got him into trouble. He was executed by Herod Antipas because he condemned Herod's marriage to the former wife of his own brother (Mark 6:17-29). Jesus paid the ultimate compliment to His courageous forerunner when He declared, "Among those born of women there has not risen anyone greater than John the Baptist" (Matthew 11:11). See also *Baptism of Jesus*; *Elizabeth*; *Zechariah*.

JOHN, GOSPEL OF. The fourth gospel of the New Testament known for its unique approach to the life and ministry of Jesus. John's gospel goes beyond the straight reporting of events so characteristic of the first three gospels; his purpose was to explain the deeper meaning of these events. As the last gospel to be written, John probably had access to these first three accounts, so he chose to focus on who Jesus was and why He came into the world.

Noticeably absent from John are the parables of Jesus that appear in Matthew, Mark, and Luke. In addition, John includes only a few of the short sayings of Jesus recorded by the other gospel writers. Instead, John expands on particular

J

events from Jesus's ministry, explaining their underlying theological meaning.

Two good examples of this technique are Jesus's long discussion with Nicodemus about the new birth (John 3:1–21) and His long monologue known as the high priestly prayer as His earthly ministry was drawing to a close (John 17:1-26). In this prayer Jesus summarized His mission, prayed that His disciples would remain faithful to the principles He had taught them, and expressed confidence in believers of the future who would continue His work through the church.

John's gospel also gives us a more accurate view of the length of Jesus's ministry than the books of Matthew, Mark, and Luke do. They mention only one trip of Jesus to Jerusalem to celebrate the Jewish Passover, which could lead us to believe that His earthly ministry lasted only about one year. But John's gospel makes it clear that Jesus traveled to Jerusalem on three separate occasions for the annual Passover celebration (2:13-23; 6:4-6; 12:1). This shows that His work as a teacher and healer lasted about three years. See also *Gospels*; *Synoptic Gospels*.

JONAH. See *Sign of Jonah*.

JORDAN RIVER. The major river of the land of Israel in which Jesus was baptized by John the Baptist (Mark 1:9). Thousands of Holy Land pilgrims are baptized in this river every year to symbolize their commitment to Jesus. Most are surprised when they realize the Jordan is not a large body of water. It is more like a creek than a river—very shallow and only about twenty-five feet wide in most places.

Most tourist baptisms today occur at Yardenit, a site near the spot where the Jordan exits the Sea of Galilee. The site of Jesus's baptism was probably in the lower reaches of the river in the wilderness area where John the Baptist was preaching. See also *Baptism of Jesus*; *Bethabara*; *John the Baptist*.

JOSEPH, HUSBAND OF MARY. The godly man who proceeded with plans to make the virgin Mary his wife after an angel assured him that her pregnancy was a result of the supernatural action of the Holy Spirit (Matthew 1:18-25).

While Joseph was not the biological father of Jesus, he considered Mary's firstborn his oldest son and taught Him the trade of a carpenter, or woodworker. To the people of Nazareth, where Jesus grew up and worked with Joseph, Jesus was nothing special; He was just "the son of Joseph" (John 6:42) or "the carpenter's son" (Matthew 13:55).

Mary and Joseph took Jesus with them to Jerusalem to celebrate a Jewish festival when He was twelve years old (Luke 2:41-52). After this event, Joseph is never mentioned again in the Gospels. This has led to speculation that he may have died before Jesus launched His public ministry. See also *Flight into Egypt.*

JOSEPH OF ARIMATHEA. A follower of Jesus who claimed Jesus's body from the Roman authorities and placed it in his own new tomb. Nicodemus helped Joseph anoint the body with spices before Jesus was entombed (John 19:38-42).

Jesus's burial by Joseph is recorded in all four gospels. Matthew calls him "a rich man" (Matthew 27:57); Mark says he was "a prominent member of the Council," or Jewish Sanhedrin (Mark 15:43); Luke describes him as "a good and upright man" (Luke 23:50); and John tells us He followed Jesus but "secretly because he feared the Jewish leaders" (John 19:38). Perhaps it was this fear that prevented Joseph from stepping forward to defend Jesus when He appeared before the Jewish high court.

But Joseph emerged from the shadows when he was needed most. He will always be remembered as the reluctant follower who gave Jesus a decent burial—something the Lord's eleven disciples were not rich enough or brave enough to do.

J

Jesus's burial in Joseph's tomb fulfilled the prophecy of Isaiah that the Messiah would be "with the rich in his death" (Isaiah 53:9). See also *Messianic Prophecies*.

JOT AND TITTLE. See *Words Will Never Pass Away*.

JUDAS, HALF BROTHER OF JESUS. One of the four brothers of Jesus born to Mary by natural means after Jesus's supernatural conception (Mark 6:3). Like his brother James, Judas did not initially believe that Jesus was God's messenger. But he may have had a change of heart after Jesus's death and resurrection.

The apostle Paul mentioned "the Lord's brothers" along with Peter and the other apostles who were doing the Lord's work (1 Corinthians 9:5-6). Some scholars believe Judas was the author of the epistle of Jude in the New Testament. See also *Brothers of Jesus*.

JUDAS ISCARIOT. A disciple of Jesus who will always be remembered as the despicable character who betrayed Jesus to His enemies by identifying Him with a kiss (Matthew 26:47-49). *Iscariot* is a form of Kerioth, the name of his hometown in the southern part of Israel, thus his designation as "Judas of Kerioth."

Judas was apparently at first a loyal disciple, even being entrusted with keeping the common funds that supported Jesus and the Twelve (John 12:6; 13:29). But He eventually turned against Jesus and agreed to deliver Him to the Jewish Sanhedrin for thirty pieces of silver (Matthew 26:15). This sum was the standard price of a slave in Bible times (Exodus 21:32).

On the night that Jesus ate the last supper with His disciples, He predicted that one of them would turn against Him. They were very sad and began to say to Him one after the other, "Surely you don't mean me, Lord?" (Matthew 26:22). Jesus clearly identified the betrayer by dipping a piece of bread in a dish and handing it to Judas (John 13:26).

Many people have wondered why Judas betrayed Jesus. Did he hope to force Jesus to use His power to bring about an earthly kingdom? Was he determined to "cash in" for himself when he realized Jesus was headed for disaster? No one knows his exact motivation, so perhaps the best reason for his action appears in Luke's gospel: "Satan entered Judas" (Luke 22:3). See also *Disciples of Jesus*; *Field of Blood*.

JUDAS, SON OF JAMES. See *Thaddaeus*.

JUDEA. The southernmost region of the land of Israel in New Testament times. It included the city of Jerusalem and its surrounding area (Matthew 3:5). Judea was the heart of the Jewish religious establishment, so it was where Jesus met fierce opposition from the Pharisees and other leaders.

The other two main regions of Israel were the northernmost area known as Galilee and the territory of Samaria that lay between Judea and Galilee. Jesus spent most of His ministry in Galilee.

Over the course of His ministry, Jesus realized that His enemies in Judea were growing more and more determined to put Him to death. He predicted as much to His disciples before His final trip to the Holy City to celebrate the Jewish Passover (Matthew 16:21).

JUDGING OTHERS. See *Sermon on the Mount*, No. 5.

KEYS OF THE KINGDOM OF HEAVEN. A phrase of Jesus that symbolized His delegation of authority to His disciples to do His work in His name. He made this statement

J

K

MAJOR EVENTS OF JESUS'S LIFE

Annunciation of Jesus's Birth

Appearances of Jesus after His Resurrection

Ascends into Heaven

Baptism of Jesus

Birth of Jesus

Childhood of Jesus

Crucifixion

Death of Jesus

Preexistence of Jesus

Resurrected from the Dead

Temptations of Jesus

Transfiguration of Jesus

Trials of Jesus

Triumphal Entry into Jerusalem

after Peter made his great confession that Jesus was the Messiah, the "Son of the living God" (Matthew 16:16).

In Jesus's time, a key was a symbol of power and authority. He spoke metaphorically to show that His own authority as God's agent of redemption would rest on His twelve disciples. Jesus had trained them personally, and they would carry on the work that God had sent Him into the world to do.

After Jesus's ascension to God the Father, His disciples became the nucleus of the early church that blossomed first in Jerusalem and then spread quickly throughout the Mediterranean world. The church, under the authority of Jesus, is still the channel through which the gospel is proclaimed to sinful humankind. See also *Great Commission*; *Head of the Church*.

KING. See *Offices of Christ*.

KINGDOM OF GOD.

God's rule of grace in human affairs, and the new world

order that Jesus came to establish (Mark 1:15). Through His teaching and healing ministry, Jesus made it clear that He was the full expression of this kingdom (Matthew 12:28). This spiritual realm is also referred to as the kingdom of heaven (Matthew 16:19).

The kingdom of God becomes a personal spiritual reality when people repent of their sin, receive forgiveness, and begin to show through their actions that they love and obey God. When the doubting Pharisees questioned Jesus about the nature of this kingdom, He declared, "The kingdom of God is in your midst" (Luke 17:21). He probably meant that every person had the potential to enter the kingdom, but only those who accept Him in faith could do so.

Jesus emphasized that the kingdom of God exists in two different dimensions—present and future. This new world order was present already in His person. But it would be realized perfectly at the end of the age when He returns in glory (Luke 17:20-37).

Jesus taught His followers to "seek first" God's kingdom, putting it above all earthly concerns, and He would provide for their material needs (Matthew 6:33). This promise provides welcome relief from the anxiety and worry that afflict a fallen world. See also *Kingdom of God Parables*.

KINGDOM OF GOD PARABLES. A string of seven parables told by Jesus to help people grasp the meaning of the kingdom of God (Matthew 13:1-52). This kingdom—also referred to as the kingdom of heaven—refers to God's rule of grace in the world, a period foretold by the Old Testament prophets. The dawning of this kingdom occurred when Jesus was born into the world.

Sower and soils (verses 1-9). In this parable, a farmer sowed seed on different types of soil. The seeds failed to grow on rocky, hardened ground, but they flourished on good soil and produced a bountiful harvest. This symbolized the proclamation of the good news about God's love and grace. Some people would reject

K

the message, but others would accept it and receive bountiful blessings from the Lord.

Wheat and weeds (verses 24–30). These two items, growing together in the same field, show that kingdom citizens as well as unbelievers will exist together in this life. But in the final judgment, God will separate them and send each group to their appropriate reward. The parable of a **fishing net** (verses 47–50), depicted as hauling in both edible and worthless fish, expresses the same message.

Two other parables of the kingdom of heaven declared its great value. A man discovered a **buried treasure** (verse 44), so he bought the property to lay claim to the valuable item. Likewise, a merchant looking for a **fine pearl** (verses 45–46; *pearl of great price:* KJV) sold everything he had in order to buy one of exceedingly great value. These parables declare that people should be willing to pay any price and make any sacrifice to claim the riches of the kingdom of God.

Two final parables emphasized the potential of God's kingdom. Jesus compared it to a tiny **mustard seed** (verses 31–32) that grew into a huge tree, and a tiny bit of **yeast** (verse 33; *leaven:* KJV) that spread throughout a lump of dough and caused it to rise. In the beginning, God's kingdom in the person of Jesus was tiny and its truths were revealed to just a few people in an isolated corner of the Mediterranean world. But this kingdom would eventually grow into a mighty force and influence all humankind. This is exactly what has happened as Christianity has grown into one of the major world religions. See also *Kingdom of God; Parables of Jesus.*

K

KING OF KINGS. See *Lord of Lords.*

KISS OF BETRAYAL. See *Judas Iscariot.*

KORAZIN. See *Chorazin.*

LAMB OF GOD. A name of Jesus used by John the Baptist, foretelling the Lord's death as a sacrifice for the sins of humankind. John, forerunner of Jesus, compared Him to the young lamb used as a sacrificial offering to atone for sin in Jewish worship rituals (John 1:29–36).

In a messianic prophecy of the Old Testament, Isaiah predicted that the Messiah would give His life like a sacrificial lamb: "He was led like a lamb to the slaughter," Isaiah declared, "and as a sheep before its shearers is silent, so he did not open his mouth" (Isaiah 53:7). This prophecy was fulfilled when Jesus refused to defend himself in His appearances before Herod Antipas (Luke 23:9) and Pilate (Mark 15:3–5).

Lambs were particularly associated with the Jewish festival known as Passover. Just before the exodus from Egypt, the Israelites spread the blood of sacrificial lambs on the doorframes of their houses. Because of this, they were "passed over" when the Lord destroyed all the firstborn among the Egyptians (Exodus 12:1–13).

Since Jesus's crucifixion occurred during a Passover celebration, early believers drew a parallel between His death and the sacrifice of a lamb during this festival. The apostle Paul picked up on this imagery when he declared, "Christ, our Passover lamb, has been sacrificed" (1 Corinthians 5:7). See also *Feast of Passover*.

LAME MAN HEALED ON THE SABBATH. Jesus went to a spring-fed pool in Jerusalem known as the Pool of Bethesda. Disabled people gathered around this pool because they thought its waters had magical healing properties. According to a popular legend, the first person to enter the water after an angel stirred it—causing it to bubble—would be healed (John 5:1–8).

Jesus noticed one particular disabled man who lay by the spring in hopes of being healed. He had been going there for thirty-eight years, but because of his limited mobility, he had not

L

been able to enter the water first after it bubbled. In an act of compassion, Jesus healed the man of his disability.

This act of mercy kindled the Pharisees' wrath against Jesus, because He had healed the man on the Sabbath. To the Jewish leaders, it was a violation of the Old Testament law against working on this sacred day.

Jesus answered their criticism with a long speech about His relationship to God the Father (John 5:19-47). He declared this act of healing was part of God's continuing work in the world. The Father had given Jesus authority to do God's work—even on the Sabbath—because of His credentials as God's Son. See also *Pool of Bethesda*.

LAMENTS OVER JERUSALEM. Near the end of His public ministry, Jesus was deeply moved by the unbelief of the people of Jerusalem. "Jerusalem, Jerusalem," He cried, "how often I have longed to gather your children together, as a hen gathers her chicks under her wings, and you were not willing" (Luke 13:34).

Jerusalem was the religious center of the Jewish people, so Jesus may have been speaking metaphorically. Most of the nation, represented by this city, had rejected His message and refused to accept Him as the Son of God. See also *Jerusalem*.

LAMP ON A LAMPSTAND PARABLE. In this brief parable, Jesus referred to the small oil-burning lamps that were used in Bible times. No homeowner would light one of these lamps and place it under a basket or a bed. It should be placed on a lampstand so it could illuminate a room (Matthew 5:15-16).

Jesus was saying that members of the kingdom of God are like lighted lamps: their function is to send the light of God's love into the lives of others. See also *Sermon on the Mount*, No. 1.

LAST ADAM. A name of Jesus that portrays Him as the antidote to the sinful state that humankind inherited from the first Adam in the book of Genesis. The apostle Paul discusses this concept in the book of 1 Corinthians (15:20-49).

According to Paul, Adam's disobedience of God in the garden of Eden infected him and his descendants with the curse of sin and death. Everyone from Adam's time throughout the rest of human history—everyone except for Jesus, that is—suffers from the malady of sin and rebellion against God. As Paul put in in the book of Romans, "All have sinned and fall short of the glory of God" (Romans 3:23).

But the good news is that God has provided a remedy for this universal ailment through the person of Jesus Christ, the last Adam. "For as in Adam all die," Paul declared, "so in Christ all will be made alive" (1 Corinthians 15:22). Jesus's perfect obedience to God the Father and His sacrificial death on the cross has canceled out the first Adam's legacy of sin and death.

NAMES AND TITLES OF JESUS

Advocate
Alpha and Omega
Author and Perfecter of Faith
Bread of Life
Bright Morning Star
Carpenter
Christ
Cornerstone
Firstborn from among the Dead
Good Shepherd
Head of the Church
Immanuel
Lamb of God
Last Adam
Light of the World
Lion of the Tribe of Judah
Lord of Lords
Mediator
Messiah
Nazarene
One and Only Son
Rabbi
Redeemer
Son of Abraham
Son of David
Son of Man
Star Out of Jacob
True Vine
Wonderful Counselor

LAST SUPPER. See *Lord's Supper.*

LAST WILL BE FIRST. See *Humble Will Be Exalted.*

LAWYER. See *Expert in the Law.*

LAZARUS AND RICH MAN PARABLE. See *Rich Man and Lazarus Parable.*

LAZARUS RAISED FROM THE DEAD. Once, when Jesus was ministering some distance from Bethany, the village where His friend Lazarus lived, the man's sisters, Mary and Martha, sent word that their brother was desperately ill. Jesus seemed unconcerned; He waited two days before setting out for the town (John 11:1–44).

When Jesus finally arrived, He learned that Lazarus had died four days before and was already in the grave. Martha greeted Him with a gentle rebuke: "Lord, if You had been here, my brother wouldn't have died" (verse 21 HCSB).

Jesus assured Martha that it was not too late for a miracle. He was "the resurrection and the life" (verse 25), and He held the keys to life and death and the promise of eternal life for all who placed their faith in Him.

Then Mary came out to meet Jesus, sobbing the same words as her sister had—that He should have been there to heal Lazarus before he died. When Jesus saw Mary's tears and heard the cries of other mourners on the scene, He was overcome with emotion. As "Jesus wept" (verse 35), He mingled His tears with theirs in a display of His true humanity. He understands people's grief, and He identifies with people's sadness and sense of loss in the death of those who are dear.

L

Then Jesus raised Lazarus from the dead with a simple command, "Lazarus, come out!" (verse 43). This was a dramatic demonstration of His power over death and the grave.

See also *Bethany; Mary, Sister of Lazarus; Martha.*

LEAVEN PARABLE. See *Kingdom of God Parables.*

LEBBAEUS. See *Thaddaeus.*

LEGION. See *Demons and Demon Possession,* No. 1.

LEPROSY. A general term for several different types of diseases of the skin in Bible times. These maladies began as sores or scabs on the skin, and sometimes resulted in the loss of fingers and toes in those who suffered the most debilitating form of these afflictions.

People with this disease were quarantined from the rest of society; they had to warn people to keep a safe distance away. But Jesus was not afraid to associate with them. The Gospels contain two accounts of His miraculous healing of people with this disability.

Jesus healed one man with a skin disease by touching him (Matthew 8:1-4). Then He told the man to take an offering and show himself to a priest. According to Old Testament law, this was a requirement before a person could be pronounced free of the disease (Leviticus 14:1-7). This declaration would allow the healed man to associate once again with his relatives and friends.

Jesus healed ten other people with leprosy by assuring them from a distance that they had been restored to health (Luke 17:11-19). He also told them to show themselves to a priest so they could be declared well. Nine of the men walked away; only one fell at Jesus's feet to thank Him for the healing.

L

This man was a Samaritan, and Jesus asked, "Where are the other nine? Has no one returned to give praise to God except this foreigner?" (verses 17-18). Then Jesus declared that the man's faith had made him spiritually clean. This event signified the rejection of Jesus by His own people, the Jews, and the ultimate acceptance of the gospel by Gentiles.

LET THE CHILDREN COME TO ME. See *Children Received by Jesus.*

LEVI. See *Matthew.*

LIFE IS MORE THAN FOOD. A phrase that Jesus used to caution believers against taking a strictly materialistic view of life (Luke 12:23). Earthly necessities such as food and clothing are important, but providing these for ourselves and our families should not be our ultimate goal in life. Our main focus should be serving God and living by the spiritual values of His kingdom. See also *Possessions*; *Treasures in Heaven.*

LIGHT OF THE WORLD. A title that Jesus used for himself (John 8:12), representing the fulfillment of Old Testament prophecy. Several centuries before Jesus was born, the prophet Isaiah predicted that a great light would shine in Galilee, bringing illumination and understanding into a dark world: "On those living in the land of deep darkness a light has dawned" (Isaiah 9:2; see Matthew 4:14-16).

As the light of the world, Jesus symbolizes the presence of God (Exodus 13:21-22), good in contrast to evil (Isaiah 5:20), salvation from sin into new life (Matthew 4:16), and guidance for life (Psalm 119:105).

LIGHT UNDER A BUSHEL. See *Sermon on the Mount,* No. 1.

LION OF THE TRIBE OF JUDAH.

LION OF THE TRIBE OF JUDAH. A name of Jesus in Revelation 5:5 that considers Him the fulfillment of an ancient prophecy about Israel's tribe of Judah. When the Old Testament patriarch Jacob blessed his twelve sons, he predicted that Judah's descendants would become the greatest of the twelve tribes that would make up the nation of Israel. Jacob, whom God renamed Israel, described Judah metaphorically as a lion, or a strong ruler, who would lead God's people (Genesis 49:8–9).

Later biblical events proved this prophecy to be true. For example, Judah's descendants grew into the largest tribe of Israel (Numbers 1:27; 26:22). And King David, a national hero and the most popular king in the nation's history, was a member of this tribe.

But the most important thing about this prophecy is that it was fulfilled when Jesus the Messiah was born into the world. The gospel of Matthew traces His family line back through several generations to Judah himself (Matthew 1:2–16).

In the apostle John's vision in the book of Revelation, this title of Jesus has implications for the day when God will bring the world to its appointed end. Only Jesus, as the lion of the tribe of Judah, is worthy to open the scroll of God's judgment (Revelation 5:9–10). God the Father has delegated to Jesus alone the authority and power to act as the final judge over all things.

LORD OF LORDS. A name of Jesus that emphasizes the victory He will have over all enemies when He returns to earth as the supreme ruler of creation. In one of his visions in the book of Revelation, the apostle John described Jesus in the end time as riding a white horse, overcoming His enemies, and judging the earth with justice and righteousness. This name, Lord of

OLD TESTAMENT PROPHECIES AND FIGURES IN THE STORY OF JESUS

Lords, will be written on His robe and His thigh (Revelation 19:11–18).

This name is actually part of a double name that John envisioned: he described Jesus as King of Kings as well as Lord of Lords. These two names leave no doubt that Jesus will return with power and authority that will make Him superior to all the rulers of the world.

LORD OF THE SABBATH. See *Sabbath.*

LORD'S DAY. The first day of the week, or Sunday. Because Jesus was resurrected from the dead on this day, the early church adopted Sunday as its day of worship (1 Corinthians 16:2). This custom continues today in most Christian traditions.

In Old Testament times, the seventh day of the week—Saturday—was the designated time for worship. To the Jewish people, this twenty-four-hour period known as the Sabbath memorialized the day on which God rested after His creation of the world (Genesis 2:2).

The apostle John's series of visions about the end time began when he was in the spirit "on the Lord's Day" (Revelation 1:10). Some interpreters see this as a direct challenge to the Roman custom of emperor worship, which may have been observed on the first day of the week. Thus, John declared that this day belonged to the Lord Jesus, not to the pagan Roman emperor. See also *Sabbath*.

LORD'S PRAYER. The model prayer that Jesus taught His disciples in response to their request, "Lord, teach us to pray" (Luke 11:1). The full version of this prayer appears in Jesus's Sermon on the Mount in the gospel of Matthew (6:9–13), while a shorter version appears in Luke's gospel (11:2–4).

In this model prayer, Jesus taught believers that we should begin our prayers by recognizing God as our heavenly Father, by honoring His name, and by asking for His kingdom to reign on earth. We should also ask Him to provide for our physical needs by giving us each day "our daily bread" (Matthew 6:11).

Every prayer we pray should also include our request for God to forgive our sins, and for us to have a forgiving spirit toward others. Genuine prayer leads us to recognize that our tendency toward wrongdoing is strong, and that we need God's strength and guidance to keep us from yielding to temptation.

This prayer from the lips of Jesus is memorialized today in a shrine known as the Church of the Pater Noster on Jerusalem's Mount of Olives. The name comes from the first two words of the prayer in Latin—*Pater Noster* ("our Father"). On the walls of the church are tiles that display the words of this famous prayer in more than fifty languages. See also *Prayer*.

L

LORD'S SUPPER. Jesus's final meal with His disciples on the night before He was arrested and crucified. This meal is also referred to as the Last Supper and the Memorial Supper.

An account of this event appears in all four gospels (Matthew 26:26–29; Mark 14:22–25; Luke 22:19–20; John 13:1–17). Jesus explained to His disciples that the bread and wine in the meal symbolized His broken and bleeding body. They were to remember the sacrifice He made for sinful humankind by celebrating this meal as a permanent ritual in future years.

In the middle of this meal, Jesus shocked His disciples by predicting that one of them would betray Him to His enemies. All of them declared they would never do such a thing. Jesus then clearly identified Judas as the betrayer (Matthew 26:20–25).

Jesus also declared that each of the disciples would abandon Him before the night was over. In spite of their strong protests, that is exactly what happened when the Jewish Sanhedrin had Jesus arrested in the garden of Gethsemane (Mark 14:50). As predicted, Peter—who declared his loyalty more vehemently than the others—actually denied Jesus three times (Mark 14:66–72). The crowing of a rooster at his third denial fulfilled Jesus's prediction. It also made Peter realize how woefully he had failed his Lord.

The Lord's Supper is still observed by believers of many different church groups throughout the world as a memorial of Jesus's sacrificial death. This ritual is also referred to as Communion, the Eucharist, and the Mass. See also *Feast of Passover*; *Upper Room*.

LOST COIN AND LOST SHEEP PARABLES. The fifteenth chapter of Luke contains back-to-back parables about three lost items—a coin, a sheep, and a son. Jesus told these parables in response to the criticism of several Pharisees and teachers of the law. They condemned Him for associating with people whom they considered outcasts and sinners (Luke 15:1–32).

In the parable of the lost sheep, Jesus asked His critics to think about a shepherd who owned one hundred sheep. If one of these sheep strayed away from the flock, wouldn't the shepherd search diligently for the wayward animal until he found it?

And, Jesus asked the Pharisees, what about a woman who owned ten silver coins? If she lost one of them, wouldn't she search carefully in every corner of her house until she found the precious coin?

Then Jesus drove home the point of these two parables, noting that the friends of the shepherd and the woman rejoiced with them when they recovered their missing property. This pointed to the love of the heavenly Father, who celebrated with great joy "over one sinner who repents" (verse 10).

Jesus took the criticism of these religious leaders as a compliment. He had been sent by His Father to gather all people—even lost sinners and despised outcasts—into the kingdom of God.

The account of the lost son in this series of three parables is better known as the parable of the prodigal son. See *Prodigal Son Parable*.

LUKE, GOSPEL OF. The third of the four gospels of the New Testament and the only one written by a person of Gentile background. Luke wrote his gospel to show that Jesus was the universal Savior who welcomed people of all backgrounds—Jews (13:34), "respectable people" (11:37), Samaritans (9:51-56), pagan Gentiles (4:25-27), tax collectors, sinners, outcasts (5:27-32), the poor (6:20), and, truly, "all people" (2:10).

Luke also highlights Jesus's inclusive attitude toward women—the widow of Nain (7:11-14), a sinful woman who anointed Him (7:36-50), and the woman with an issue of blood whom He healed (8:42-48). God the Father even inspired Luke to record the prophetess Anna's experience with the baby Jesus in the temple (2:36-38).

Luke was a physician who accompanied the apostle Paul on several of his missionary tours (Acts 27:1-28:16). His gospel is the first part of a two-part work known as Luke-Acts that he dedicated to his friend Theophilus (Luke 1:3; Acts 1:1). See also *Gospels*; *Synoptic Gospels*.

LUSTING IN ONE'S HEART. See *Adultery*.

MAGADAN. A region along the shore of the Sea of Galilee where Jesus withdrew with His disciples after the miraculous feeding of the four thousand (Matthew 15:39; *Magdala:* KJV). It was probably the home of Mary Magdalene ("Mary of Magdala"), a woman out of whom Jesus cast seven demons, and who became one of His followers (Luke 8:1-4).

During the time of Jesus, Magadan was a prosperous fishing village. At this location, fish caught in the Sea of Galilee were probably processed and shipped to points throughout Israel.

In a modern museum not far from the site of ancient Magadan are the remains of a wooden boat that has been dated to the first century AD. Dubbed the "Jesus Boat" by Holy Land pilgrims, it was pulled from the mud just off the shore of the Sea of Galilee in 1986. But experts aren't sure if this is a fishing boat from Jesus's time or perhaps a ferry or even a Roman warship.

Mark's gospel refers to Magadan as Dalmanutha (Mark 8:10). See also *Mary Magdalene*.

MAGI. Astrologers from a far eastern country, perhaps Babylon or Persia, who traveled hundreds of miles to honor the infant Jesus soon after He was born in Bethlehem (Matthew 2:1-12; *wise men:* KJV).

These foreigners were members of a priestly caste who studied the heavenly bodies for signs that foretold the destiny of nations as well as individuals. When the Magi saw a strange star in the sky, they interpreted this as a sign that a new king of the Jewish people had been born.

L

M

After a stop in Jerusalem, they were directed to the village of Bethlehem, just a few miles away. Here they found Mary and Joseph and the infant Jesus, whom they presented with gifts of gold, incense, and myrrh.

A popular Christmas carol, "We Three Kings of Orient Are," identify the Magi as royal rulers of a specific number—probably because of the three gifts they brought. But the Bible does not tell us how many people made the trip or that they were kings.

Another interesting thing about the Magi's visit is that they found the infant Jesus and His parents in a house (verse 11). Mary and Joseph had left the Bethlehem stable for a more permanent dwelling by the time their visitors arrived. King Herod tried to eliminate the young Jesus by issuing a death order against all male infants in the region who were "two years old and under" (Matthew 2:16). These facts suggest that the Magi made their visit to Bethlehem when Jesus was about two years of age.

The main message of the Magi's visit is that Jesus's birth had worldwide significance. Soon after He was born into the world, He was worshiped by people from a far country as one destined to become a universal king. See also *Star of Bethlehem*.

MAGNIFICAT. A song of praise to God, offered by the virgin Mary after she was greeted by her relative Elizabeth (Luke 1:46-55). This happened a few months before Mary gave birth to Jesus, the promised Messiah. In Latin the song begins with the word *magnificat*, meaning "magnify." Mary praised the Lord for remembering "the humble state of his servant" (verse 48) and for keeping His promise to bless His people. See also *Mary, Mother of Jesus*.

M

MALCHUS'S EAR HEALED. A servant of the high priest came with the crowd of Jewish authorities who arrested Jesus, and according to the gospel of John, his name was Malchus. Jesus's disciple Peter drew his sword and struck a glancing blow on Malchus, cutting off his ear. Jesus rebuked Peter for resorting to violence, declared that His arrest was part of God's plan for His redemptive death (John 18:10-11).

The gospel of Luke tells us that Jesus restored Malchus's severed ear (Luke 22:47-51). Jesus was in control of the situation—even in this chaotic hour, He found the divine strength to love His enemies.

MALEFACTOR. See *Thief on the Cross.*

MAMMON. See *Possessions.*

MAN BORN BLIND HEALED. Jesus healed a man who had been blind his entire life by mixing His saliva with dirt and rubbing it on the man's eyes (John 9:1-41). This seems gross and unsanitary to the modern mind, but some people of Jesus's time believed that common spit, especially that of a famous person, had certain magical qualities.

Perhaps this man had heard about Jesus, but he couldn't see Him. The man could feel the warm mud as Jesus applied it to his sightless eyes. When he washed in the nearby Pool of Siloam at Jesus's command, the formerly blind man could suddenly see for the first time in his life.

When the Pharisees heard about this healing, they denied it had happened and even tried to discredit the man and his account of the miracle. They insisted that Jesus could not perform such miracles, since they considered Him a sinner and a lawbreaker. But the man stuck with his testimony, which was hard to refute:

M

"I don't know whether he is a sinner," he told them. "But I know this: I was blind, and now I can see!" (verse 25 NLT).

Jesus's saliva played a role in two other healing miracles. See also *Blind Man Healed at Bethsaida*; *Deaf Man with Speech Impediment Healed*.

MAN IN THE SYNAGOGUE HEALED. See *Demons and Demon Possession*, No. 4.

MAN WITH BODY FLUID HEALED. On one particular Sabbath, Jesus was dining in the home of a prominent Pharisee. Several of this man's pharisaic friends were keeping a close eye on Jesus to see if they could catch Him doing something they considered unlawful (Luke 14:1-6).

Right in front of Jesus was a man who suffered from a build-up of fluid in his body (*dropsy:* KJV). Knowing the extreme views on the Sabbath held by the Pharisees, He asked them whether it would be against the law for Him to heal the man. Their refusal to answer showed that Jesus had turned their question back on them.

If the Pharisees answered that such a healing broke the law, they would be considered hard-hearted and uncaring. But if they replied that Sabbath healing was okay, they would be guilty of going against their own teachings.

Jesus proceeded to heal the man, and went on to expose their hypocrisy. These Pharisees would certainly pull their ox out of a pit if it fell in on the Sabbath (verse 5). Thus, Jesus declared that human need was more important than the mindless and legalistic following of the Old Testament law. See also *Sabbath*.

MAN WITH DEFORMED HAND HEALED. This miracle is similar to another of Jesus's healing miracles (see *Man with Body Fluid Healed*). The Lord performed both miracles on the

M

OPPONENTS OF JESUS

Annas

Antichrist

Beelzebul

Caiaphas

Chief Priests

Devil

Expert in the Law

Herod, No. 1

Herodians

Judas Iscariot

Pharisees

Pilate

Sadducees

Sanhedrin

Satan

Sabbath as a direct challenge to the Pharisees and their legalistic rules on Sabbath observance (Luke 6:6-11).

Jesus healed the man with a deformed hand in the synagogue where He was teaching before a crowd. This public challenge to the Sabbath law infuriated the scribes and Pharisees and made them even more determined to have Him arrested and put to death.

MAN WITH LEPROSY HEALED. See *Leprosy*.

MANGER. See *Bethlehem*.

MARK, GOSPEL OF. The shortest of the four gospels and probably the first to be written. Mark established the pattern used by the gospels of Matthew and Luke. They followed Mark's lead at many points, often adding more details to his concise accounts.

Mark has been called the gospel of action. He portrays Jesus as constantly on the move, healing people and confronting others with the claims of the kingdom of God. Mark sees Jesus as a person known more for what He does than what He says.

Mark also shows the human side of Jesus's nature more pointedly than any other gospel. Jesus displays anger (11:15-17), disappointment (8:12), amazement (6:6), and even fatigue (4:38). Jesus felt every human emotion, so He is a Savior who identifies with us in our daily struggles. See also *Gospels*; *Synoptic Gospels*.

MARRIAGE AND DIVORCE. While Jesus was teaching the crowds, a group of Pharisees approached Him with a trick question. They asked, "Is it lawful for a man to divorce his wife for any and every reason?" (Matthew 19:3).

They were probably trying to get Jesus to choose between the two views of marriage and divorce that were popular at the time. Some rabbis taught that a man could divorce his wife only if she had been unfaithful to him. Other Jewish officials took a more liberal approach to the issue, saying that a man could end his relationship with his wife for any flippant reason—even if she burned his dinner or failed to please him with how she dressed. No matter how Jesus responded to the question, these Pharisees figured, He would alienate some people in the crowd.

But Jesus surprised His enemies by referring them to the account of the garden of Eden in the Old Testament. God created Adam and Eve for each other, He noted, and brought them together in a one-flesh relationship (Genesis 2:21-24). God's ideal was for this union not to be broken for any reason: "What God has joined together," Jesus declared, "let no one separate" (Matthew 19:6).

The Pharisees pressed the question. If that was true, they wanted to know, then why did Moses make allowance for divorce in the Old Testament, as cited clearly in Deuteronomy 24:1-4?

M

Jesus replied that the Mosaic law allowed for divorce only because the Jewish people found it difficult to accept the principle of marriage to one person for a lifetime. He went on to state that marital unfaithfulness by one of the marriage partners was the sole exception to this no-divorce ideal.

Any study of Jesus's teaching on this subject should consider His example of love and forgiveness toward those whose marriage and family life was less than ideal. See also *Adultery*; *Woman at the Well*.

MARTHA. The woman whom Jesus gently rebuked for being too busy to spend time with Him (Luke 10:38-42). Jesus often visited in the home of Martha, her sister Mary, and their brother Lazarus in the village of Bethany near Jerusalem. During one of these visits, Martha was busy like a good hostess, perhaps fixing a meal for her hungry guest. You can imagine her frustration when Mary didn't lift a finger to help. Mary was visiting with Jesus and listening to His teaching.

Martha took her complaints straight to Jesus. But He pointed out that Martha was busy about many frivolous things, while Mary had chosen to talk with Jesus—the "one thing" that was needed in that situation. Perhaps Jesus was saying that Martha did not have to worry about setting an elaborate table—serving a simple meal would free up both sisters to spend some quiet moments with Him.

Near the end of Jesus's earthly ministry, Lazarus died. Martha went out to meet Jesus as soon as He arrived at their home. She expressed her disappointment that He had not been there to heal Lazarus before his death. Jesus assured Martha that her brother would live again because He had the power to bring Lazarus back to life (John 11:17-44).

Martha's response to this claim is one of the strongest affirmations of faith in the Gospels: "Lord, I believe that you are the Messiah, the Son of God, who is to come into the world" (verse 27). Jesus then raised Lazarus from the dead. See also *Lazarus Raised from the Dead*; *Mary, Sister of Lazarus*.

M

MARY MAGDALENE. A woman from the village of Magadan, or Magdala, who was healed of demon possession by Jesus and who became one of His most loyal followers (Luke 8:1–3). Unlike His disciples, who fled the scene, she followed Jesus all the way to the crucifixion site. Then she stood near the cross with Jesus's mother and other women, possibly to comfort Him in His hour of suffering (Matthew 27:55–56).

Mary Magdalene, along with another woman named Mary, also watched as Joseph of Arimathea buried Jesus's body in his own new tomb (Matthew 27:57–61). She returned to the tomb on Sunday morning with this same woman to finish anointing His body with spices. Here, they encountered an angel with the startling news that Jesus had been raised from the dead (Matthew 28:1–7).

The four gospels differ in their accounts of which women visited the tomb, how many there were, exactly how angels assured them that Jesus was alive, and how the disciples were told that Jesus had been resurrected. Only John's gospel records that Mary Magdalene lingered at the empty tomb after everyone else had inspected it and then left the scene. Jesus rewarded Mary's faithfulness by appearing to her in His resurrection body. He directed her to tell His disciples that she had actually seen Him alive (John 20:1–18).

So Mary Magdalene, according to the gospel of John, was the first person to see Jesus in His resurrection body after His victory over death and the grave. Jesus also appeared to His disciples that same day—as if they needed to see for themselves that Mary's report was true (John 20:19–20).

Mary Magdalene has been the object of endless speculation. Some have tried to identify her as the sinful woman who anointed Jesus's feet with expensive perfume (Mark 14:3). Others think she was the woman accused of adultery whom Jesus forgave (John 8:1–11). But there is no evidence to support either of these claims. See also *Magadan*.

M

MARY, MOTHER OF JESUS. A young woman from Nazareth who was divinely chosen to give birth to the Messiah. Mary was informed by the angel Gabriel that, while still a virgin, she would conceive a child through the action of the Holy Spirit. This child would grow up like any Jewish boy, but would eventually be known as the "Son of the Most High" (Luke 1:32).

Mary, who was engaged to be married to a man named Joseph, was puzzled by the news. "How will this be," Mary asked the angel, "since I am a virgin?" (verse 34). But after reassurance from Gabriel, she accepted her role as "the Lord's servant" (verse 38). Later, Mary praised the Lord for the great honor of bearing this child, whom God would use to bless the nation of Israel as well as the rest of the world (Luke 1:46-55).

After this brief introduction to Mary in Luke's gospel, she is mentioned only a few times by the gospel writers. She gave birth to Jesus in Bethlehem (Luke 2:1-7), presented Him as an infant in the temple in Jerusalem (Luke 2:21-24), fled with Joseph and Jesus to Egypt to escape Herod the Great's death order (Matthew 2:13-15), returned from Egypt and settled in Nazareth (Matthew 2:19-23), attended a wedding where Jesus turned water into wine (John 2:1-3), and looked on as her first-born child was crucified (John 19:26).

Some church groups revere Mary as the "mother of God," while others ignore the important role she played in God's decision to bring His Son into the world in human form. At the very least, we should honor her as an example of great faith and deep commitment to the will of God. See also *Virgin Birth*.

MARY, SISTER OF LAZARUS. The sister of Martha and Lazarus who anointed Jesus's feet with expensive perfume and wiped them with her hair. This may have been an expression of gratitude from Mary for raising her brother Lazarus from the dead. Jesus's disciple Judas criticized her for what he considered a wasteful act. But Jesus accepted Mary's gesture as a symbolic

M

anointing for His approaching death and burial (John 12:1-8). See also *Anointing of Jesus*; *Martha*.

MASS. See *Lord's Supper*.

MATTHEW. A tax collector who left his collection booth to become a disciple of Jesus (Matthew 9:9). Matthew then hosted a banquet to which he invited Jesus and His disciples and several of his tax collector associates (Luke 5:27-32). At this event Jesus was criticized by the Pharisees for associating with tax collectors and sinners.

Matthew was also known as Levi (Mark 2:13-14). He is the author of the gospel that bears his name. See also *Disciples of Jesus*; *Matthew, Gospel of*.

MATTHEW, GOSPEL OF. The first of the four gospels, serving as a natural bridge between the Old and New Testaments. Matthew wrote his gospel to show that Jesus was the fulfillment of Old Testament prophecy. He quoted from the Old Testament numerous times—more than any other gospel writer (for example, 10:35-36; 15:4, 8-9; 27:9-10).

Matthew also emphasizes the teachings of Jesus. He collected the essence of His teachings into a section known as the Sermon on the Mount (chapters 5-7). Here Jesus taught His disciples and other followers how to live as citizens of the kingdom of God.

Matthew's focus on this kingdom is also evident throughout the gospel, where it is mentioned nearly fifty times. The kingdom of God means the reign of God in human hearts. It offers happiness and contentment to those who give God first place in their lives. See also *Gospels*; *Synoptic Gospels*.

M

MATTHIAS. A believer chosen by Jesus's disciples to succeed Judas (Acts 1:23-26). His selection brought the number of disciples back to twelve after the betrayal and suicide of Judas. The disciples apparently thought it was essential to maintain the exact number of apostles that Jesus had originally chosen. See also *Disciples of Jesus.*

MEDIATOR. A name of Jesus that emphasizes His role as God's divine agent who bridges the gap that separates God and humankind. The name comes from the writings of the apostle Paul (1 Timothy 2:5).

God is holy and He will not tolerate anything that is impure or unclean. Human beings are His polar opposite—all people are hopelessly trapped in a state of unrighteousness that is caused by sin. But Jesus's atoning death on the cross eliminated this gap between God and humankind. Through our repentance and God's forgiveness, we are reconciled to God through the work of Jesus Christ as our Mediator.

Just as Jesus is our Mediator, He expects believers to have a part in His mediating work. Through our positive witness, we can help others find their way to joyful fellowship with God the Father. The apostle Paul put it like this: "All things are of God, who has reconciled us to Himself through Jesus Christ, and has given us the ministry of reconciliation" (2 Corinthians 5:18 NKJV).

MEEKNESS. See *Beatitudes.*

MEMORIAL SUPPER. See *Lord's Supper.*

MESSIAH. A title for the long-expected deliverer of the Jewish people. Jesus rarely applied the term to himself directly. But the

Bible records one instance, when the woman at the well told Him she believed the Messiah was coming. Jesus replied, "I, the one speaking to you—I am he" (John 4:26).

Jesus actually cautioned people not to refer to Him by this name (Matthew 16:20)—a concept referred to as the "Messianic Secret." He knew the Jewish people were expecting the Messiah to be a military hero who would restore the Jewish nation to its former glory. Jesus refused to conform to their expectations by deliberately avoiding the name. He came into the world as a different kind of deliverer—a spiritual Savior who would rescue people from their sin.

MESSIANIC PROPHECIES. Passages in the Old Testament that foretold the coming of the Messiah. These predictions were fulfilled in the life and ministry of Jesus Christ. Students of the Bible have located more than 120 Old Testament passages considered messianic in nature. Listed below are those classified as major predictions.

PROPHECY	O. T. PASSAGE	N. T. FULFILLMENT
From the lineage of David	Isa. 11:1–10	Matt. 1:1
A prophet like Moses	Deut. 18:15–19	Mark 6:14–15
Author of new covenant	Jer. 31:31–34	Heb. 12:24
Born of a virgin	Isa. 7:14	Matt. 1:18–25
Born at Bethlehem	Mic. 5:2	Luke 2:4–7
Will be called from Egypt	Hos. 11:1	Matt. 2:13–15
Named Immanuel	Isa. 7:14	Matt. 1:22–23
Forerunner to precede Him	Mal. 3:1	Mark 1:1–8
Will preach good news	Isa. 61:2–3	Luke 4:43

M

PROPHECY	O. T. PASSAGE	N. T. FULFILLMENT
Filled with God's spirit	Isa. 11:2	Matt. 3:16-17
Rejected by His own people	Isa. 53:3	John 1:11
Messenger to the Gentiles	Isa. 11:10	Rom. 15:9-12
Worker of miracles	Isa. 35:5-6	Matt. 11:4-5
Humble entry into Jerusalem	Zech. 9:9	Matt. 21:1-11
Betrayed for thirty pieces of silver	Zech. 11:12-13	Matt. 26:14-15
Silent before His accusers	Isa. 53:7	Mark 15:4-5
Put to death with criminals	Isa. 53:12	Matt. 27:38
Mocked on the cross	Ps. 22:6-8	Matt. 27:39-44
No bone broken	Ps. 34:20	John 19:32-36
Died for others	Isa. 53:1-12	1 Pet. 3:18
Buried among the rich	Isa. 53:9	Matt. 27:57-60
Ascended to His Father	Ps. 68:18	Eph. 4:8-10
Intercedes for believers	Zech. 6:13	Rom. 8:34
Exalted above all things	Ps. 2:6-12	Phil. 2:9-11

MESSIANIC SECRET. See *Messiah*.

MICAH. An Old Testament prophet who foretold the exact place where the Messiah would be born (Micah 5:2). The prophecy was fulfilled more than six centuries later when Jesus was born in Bethlehem (Matthew 2:3-6). See also *Bethlehem*; *Messianic Prophecies*.

M

MINAS PARABLE. This parable is similar to Jesus's parable of the talents. But the account of the minas (*pounds:* KJV) emphasizes the Lord's second coming, while the talents parable focuses on stewardship of gifts and abilities.

Jesus related the minas parable to a group of people who expected Him to establish the kingdom of God immediately. So He told about a man of noble birth who went to a distant country to be named a king. The period of time before this man's return as a king represented the years between Jesus's ascension into heaven and His return in glory at the end of the age (Luke 19:11-27). So, with this parable, He corrected the impression that His return was imminent.

For the interval between Jesus's ascension and His return, He assigned His followers certain responsibilities. These duties are symbolized by the differing numbers of minas—an amount of money equivalent to about three month's wages—that the future king gave His servants to manage while He was away.

Jesus ended the parable with a statement about the destruction of His enemies, those who opposed His kingship. These included many of His Jewish countrymen, as well as all people who declare through their thoughts and actions, "We don't want this man to be our king" (verse 14). See also *Second Coming; Talents Parable.*

MIRACLES OF JESUS. The miracles of Jesus in the Gospels showed His unlimited power as well as the authority that He derived from God the Father. Most of these were miracles of healing. But He also demonstrated His power over the natural order by doing such things as walking on water, calming a storm, and producing miraculous catches of fish.

Following is a complete list of all Jesus's miracles. For a brief description of each, see the appropriate article at its alphabetical listing throughout this book.

M

- Ascends into heaven
- Blind and deaf man healed
- Blind man healed at Bethsaida
- Blind Bartimaeus healed at Jericho
- Boy with seizures healed
- Calms a storm
- Centurion's servant healed
- Curses barren fig tree
- Daughter of a Gentile woman healed
- Deaf man healed
- Deaf man with speech impediment healed
- Feeds five thousand people
- Feeds four thousand Gentiles
- Jairus's daughter raised from the dead
- Lame man healed on the Sabbath
- Lazarus raised from the dead
- Malchus's ear healed
- Man born blind healed
- Man in the synagogue healed
- Man with body fluid healed
- Man with deformed hand healed
- Man with leprosy healed
- Miraculous catches of fish
- Paralyzed man healed
- Peter's mother-in-law healed
- Produces a coin for the temple tax
- Resurrected from the grave
- Royal official's son healed
- Ten men with leprosy healed
- Transfiguration of Jesus
- Turns water into wine
- Two blind men healed
- Walks on the water
- Widow's son raised from the dead
- Wild man among the tombs healed
- Woman with crooked back healed

M

- Woman with hemorrhage healed

MIRACULOUS CATCHES OF FISH. Jesus enabled His disciples to fill their nets with large catches of fish on two different occasions—both at the beginning and the end of His public ministry.

The first catch occurred when Jesus encountered the two sets of fishermen brothers—Peter and Andrew and James and John—fishing on the Sea of Galilee. They had worked all night without catching a single fish. Jesus told them to let down their nets one last time (Luke 5:1-11).

When they did so, they were astonished at the number of fish that filled their nets. This miracle demonstrated Jesus's power and convinced the four fishermen to become His disciples. Jesus told them, "From now on you will be catching people!" (verse 10 HCSB).

The second fishing miracle happened a few days after Jesus's resurrection. Several of His disciples were fishing from a boat on the Sea of Galilee when He called to them from the shore. At His command they let down their nets and hauled in a huge catch (John 21:4-6).

Jesus had built a fire and was broiling some fish. He added some of the disciples' catch to the flames and prepared breakfast for the entire group. As Jesus handed out the food, the men were reminded that Jesus had been sent into the world to serve others—and that He expected them to do the same.

MITE. See *Widow's Sacrificial Offering.*

MOCKED ON THE CROSS. See *Crucifixion.*

MODEL PRAYER. See *Lord's Prayer.*

M

PASSION AND DEATH OF JESUS

Abba

Barabbas

Caiaphas

Crucifixion of Jesus

Cup of Suffering

Death of Jesus

Gethsemane

Herod, No. 3

Joseph of Arimathea

Judas Iscariot

Lamb of God

Malchus's Ear Healed

Pilate

Resurrected from the Grave

Sanhedrin

Seven Sayings from the Cross

Simon of Cyrene

Skull, The

Stone Pavement

Thief on the Cross

Trials of Jesus

Via Dolorosa

MONEY. See *Possessions.*

MONEYCHANGERS. See *Cleanses the Temple.*

MOSES. The famous lawgiver of the Old Testament who, along with the prophet Elijah, appeared with Jesus at His transfiguration. Moses and Elijah talked with Jesus about the events that were destined to take place in Jerusalem very soon—the Lord's death and resurrection (Luke 9:28–36).

The men's appearance connected Jesus's glorification and redemptive sacrifice with the grand scheme of God's redemptive purpose that may be traced throughout the Old Testament. See also *Transfiguration of Jesus.*

MOTE IN ONE'S EYE. See *Sermon on the Mount,* No. 5.

MOTHER OF JESUS. See *Mary, Mother of Jesus.*

MOUNT HERMON. The highest mountain in Israel and the place identified by some scholars as the site where Jesus was transfigured before three of His disciples—Peter, James, and John (Matthew 17:1-8). But the place where this occurred is identified only as a "high mountain" (verse 1). Others think the more likely summit is Mount Tabor in the region of Galilee. See also *Mount Tabor.*

MOUNT OF OLIVES. A high hill just outside Jerusalem that offers a panoramic view of the Holy City. This elevated site is where Jesus was betrayed by Judas into the hands of His enemies (Matthew 26:30-47). It was named for the numerous olive trees that grew here in New Testament times.

After Jesus had driven merchants and moneychangers from the temple in Jerusalem, He retreated to the Mount of Olives. Here He entered a garden known as Gethsemane, where He ago- nized in prayer to God the Father. He sensed that His public min- istry was drawing to a close and that His crucifixion and death were just a few hours away.

After His resurrection, Jesus ascended into heaven from the Mount of Olives, near the village of Bethany (Luke 24:50-51). See also *Gethsemane.*

MOUNT OF TRANSFIGURATION. See *Mount Tabor.*

MOUNT TABOR. A mountain about ten miles southwest of the Sea of Galilee that is considered the traditional site of Jesus's transfiguration (Matthew 17:1-8). Through the centuries, several churches have been erected on this mountain to memorialize the reputed site of this miracle.

Two monasteries stand today on the ruins of these earlier buildings. Many modern Holy Land pilgrims visit the Church

M

of the Transfiguration, a shrine located on the grounds of the Catholic monastery. See also *Mount Hermon; Transfiguration of Jesus.*

MUSTARD SEED. See *Kingdom of God Parables.*

MY GOD, MY GOD, WHY HAVE YOU FORSAKEN ME? See *Seven Sayings from the Cross,* No. 5.

NAIN. A village near Jesus's hometown of Nazareth, where He raised a widow's son from the dead (Luke 7:11–17). As the Lord and His disciples entered the village, they were met by a funeral procession headed in the other direction. Jesus was moved with compassion for this poor widow because she had lost her only son—perhaps her only means of support.

An Arab village known as Nein stands today on the site of the town where this miracle occurred. A small church commemorates the miracle.

NATHANAEL. The disciple of Jesus who questioned whether the Messiah could come from a backwater town such as Nazareth. When his friend Philip told Nathanael that he had met the Messiah, the latter scoffed, "Can anything good come from there?" (John 1:46).

To his credit, Nathanael agreed to check out Philip's claim for himself. His doubt turned to faith when he learned that Jesus knew about him and his character even before they met. He confessed Jesus as the Messiah and agreed to follow Him.

After this encounter with Jesus, Nathanael is barely mentioned again in the Gospels. He is part of the group that goes fishing with Peter after Jesus's death and resurrection (John 21:1–14), and is noted in brief listings of the Twelve (Matthew 10:2–4, Mark 3:14–19,

M

N

Luke 6:12–16). These lists do not use the name Nathanael; the disciple is probably the same one noted as Bartholomew. See also *Disciples of Jesus*.

NAZARENE. A reference to Jesus as the fulfillment of Old Testament prophecy. Since He grew up in the village of Nazareth, He was called a Nazarene (Matthew 2:23).

NAZARETH. A village in the region of Galilee where Jesus spent most of His life until launching His public ministry at about the age of thirty (Luke 3:23). He was so well known to Nazareth's citizens that they refused to believe He was a messenger sent from God. "He's just a carpenter," they scoffed, "the son of Mary" (Mark 6:3 NLT). Because of this skepticism by those who knew Him best, Jesus lamented that "a prophet is not without honor except in his hometown" (Matthew 13:57 HCSB).

Nazareth was also the town where the angel Gabriel informed the virgin Mary that she would give birth to the Messiah (Luke 1:26–33). This event is memorialized by a modern church known as the Basilica of the Annunciation, reputed to stand on the very site where this dramatic announcement occurred.

Being from Nazareth did not work to Jesus's advantage in His early ministry. When future disciple Nathanael learned Jesus was from this little town, he asked, "Can anything good come from Nazareth?" (John 1:46 NLT). The people of Jesus's time apparently thought the long-expected Messiah would come from a major center of Jewish culture such as Jerusalem. But once He became well known, the common people had no problem referring to Him as "Jesus of Nazareth" (Luke 18:37).

NET. See *Kingdom of God Parables*.

N

NEW BIRTH. See *Nicodemus.*

NEW COVENANT. See *Jeremiah.*

NICODEMUS. A Pharisee and member of the Jewish Sanhedrin who talked with Jesus about the new birth early in the Lord's public ministry (John 3:1–21). Nicodemus had apparently heard about Jesus and wanted to find out firsthand about this teacher and miracle worker who had burst upon the scene.

Nicodemus was puzzled by Jesus's statement that "no one can see the kingdom of God unless they are born again" (verse 3). Jesus patiently explained that He was referring to rebirth or transformation of a person's total being through the supernatural action of God's Spirit. He went on to compare this action of the Spirit to the gentle blowing of the wind.

Jesus observed that we can't see the wind and we don't know where it comes from or where it goes, but we can hear it and see its effects. In the same way, the action of the Spirit is not something we can see or fully understand. But people who experience the Spirit's power can feel its reality. Others can also see a change in the lives of those who have experienced the new birth.

Nicodemus still didn't understand, so He asked Jesus, "How can this be?" (verse 9). He was essentially asking, how could something like the new birth happen? As a Jewish official, Nicodemus depended on keeping the law to guarantee his good standing with God. He couldn't grasp that yielding oneself to the action of the Holy Spirit was the way to find God and enter His kingdom.

Jesus answered this question by saying that He was the key to the door into the kingdom of God. The heavenly Father had sent Jesus into the world on a mission of redemption for a sin-darkened world: "God so loved the world that he gave his one and only Son, that whoever believes in him shall not perish but have eternal life" (verse 16). Believing and trusting in Jesus opens the door for the work of the Spirit, who guarantees forgiveness and makes it possible for human beings to experience eternal life.

Did Nicodemus finally grasp the truth and become a follower of Jesus? Later events in the Gospels show that he probably did, although he was hesitant to declare his loyalty openly. On one occasion before the Lord's enemies, Nicodemus came to Jesus's defense (John 7:50-51), and he worked with Joseph of Arimathea to give Jesus's body a decent burial (John 19:38-40).

NOAH. A righteous man of the Old Testament who built an ark at God's command and escaped the great flood (Genesis 6:9-7:22). Jesus compared His second coming to the conditions that existed in Noah's time: the Lord would return at a time when people least expected it, just as Noah's wicked generation was busy with their daily activities when the waters began to rise (Matthew 24:36-44).

Jesus also declared that the time of His second coming was known only to God the Father. Even He as God's Son did not know when it would happen (verse 36). In view of this uncertainty, believers should wait expectantly and be on the alert that it could happen at any time. See also *Second Coming*.

NON-RETALIATION. See *Eye for Eye*.

NO ONE CAN SERVE TWO MASTERS. See *Possessions*.

NO PLACE TO LAY HIS HEAD. See *Take Up One's Cross*.

OFFICES OF CHRIST. Jesus is known by many titles in the Old and New Testaments. These titles are often summarized by the work He accomplished through His threefold "office"

PHARISEES AND JESUS

(a special duty or position) as prophet, priest, and king.

As a prophet, Jesus was the ideal representative and spokesman of His heavenly Father to the world. His perfect obedience revealed God's character and His purpose for humankind (John 1:18).

Through His work as priest, Jesus gave His life on the cross as a once-for-all sacrifice for the sins of the world. He continues to intercede with the Father on behalf of His people (Romans 8:34).

As king, Jesus is exalted above all earthly rulers and kingdoms. The entire world is subject to His rule (Revelation 19:15–16).

OLIVET DISCOURSE.

Jesus's long monologue about future events in Matthew 24–25. The name comes from the place—the Mount of Olives—where Jesus discussed these happenings with His disciples. This passage is also referred to as Jesus's eschato-logical discourse.

This long discussion is con-fusing to some Bible students because Jesus intermingled a short-term prophecy (the destruction of the temple in Jerusalem) with two long-term prophecies (His second coming and the end times).

Most interpreters believe Jesus dealt with the destruction of the temple in Matthew 24:4–25, ending with the phrase, "See, I have told you ahead of time" (verse 25). This prophecy was fulfilled in AD 70, when the Roman army destroyed Jerusalem. The remainder of Jesus's discussion dealt with the two long-term prophecies (Matthew 24:26–25:46).

Signs of the end times mentioned by Jesus include the appearance of false Christs, widespread wars and rumors of wars, the darkening of the sun and moon, falling stars, and the second coming of Jesus himself. Since no one knows when Jesus will return, believers should watch and wait expectantly for this prophecy to be fulfilled. See also *Abomination that Causes Desolation*.

ONE AND ONLY SON. A title of Jesus that emphasizes His special relationship with God the Father. It appears in what is probably the best known verse in the Bible—John 3:16: "For God so loved the world that he gave his one and only Son, that whoever believes in him shall not perish but have eternal life" (John 3:16; *only begotten son:* KJV).

Jesus not only claimed to be God's Son; this relationship was affirmed by God the Father when He declared at Jesus's baptism, "This is my Son, whom I love; with him I am well pleased" (Matthew 3:17).

Jesus is one of a kind—the only Son of God the Father who has ever existed. The apostle John, in the very first chapter of his gospel, also described Jesus as "the one and only Son" (1:14). That God would send Jesus to be sacrificed for our sin shows that He held nothing back when He decided to redeem a fallen world.

ONLY BEGOTTEN SON.

See *One and Only Son.*

OVERSEER OF YOUR SOULS.

See *Good Shepherd.*

OWNER OF A HOUSE PARABLE. In this short parable, Jesus paid a compliment to His disciples. They had a solid understanding of the Old Testament, with its rich deposit of truth. Added to this was their grasp of new insights they had learned from His teachings.

The disciples were like the owner of a house (*householder:* KJV) "who brings out of his storeroom new treasures as well as old" (Matthew 13:52). Now they were ready to pass these truths along to others.

PARABLES OF JESUS. Stories and object lessons from daily life that Jesus used to teach spiritual truths. The word *parable* comes from a term that means "comparison" or "a casting alongside." Thus, Jesus compared familiar activities (such as sowing seed) or well-known objects (such as sheep) with the truths He was trying to get across to His audience. Common people could understand such comparisons.

Not every parable of Jesus was an extended story. He also used short parabolic sayings or "one-liners" such as "salt of the earth" and "casting pearls before swine" to communicate spiritual realities. For this reason it is difficult to pin down the exact number of His parables. If all of Jesus's short similes and metaphors are counted as parables, there are about fifty in the Gospels. But His major parables, or extended narratives, come to about half that number.

P

The following is a list of the major parables of Jesus. For the meaning of each, see the full description at the appropriate alphabetical listing throughout this book.

- Barren fig tree
- Buried treasure
- Fishing net
- Good Samaritan
- Great banquet
- House built on a rock
- Lamp on a lampstand
- Lost coin
- Lost sheep
- Minas
- Mustard seed
- Owner of a house
- Persistent widow
- Precious pearl
- Prodigal son
- Proud Pharisee
- Rich fool
- Rich man and Lazarus
- Shrewd manager
- Sower and soils
- Talents
- Ten virgins
- Two sons and a vineyard
- Unforgiving servant
- Wedding banquet
- Wheat and weeds
- Wicked tenants in a vineyard
- Workers in a vineyard
- Yeast in dough

PLACES VISITED BY JESUS

Bethany
Bethphage
Bethsaida
Caesarea Philippi
Cana
Capernaum
Chorazin
Decapolis
Emmaus
Galilee
Gethsemane
Jacob's Well
Jericho
Jerusalem
Jordan River
Judea
Magadan
Mount of Olives
Mount Tabor
Nain
Nazareth
Pool of Bethesda
Pool of Siloam
Samaria
Sychar
Upper Room

PARADOX. A statement that contradicts itself but is nevertheless true. Jesus used this technique often in His teaching. See *Find One's Life by Losing It*; *Humble Will Be Exalted*.

PARALYZED MAN HEALED. Once, while Jesus taught in a crowded house, some men came carrying a paralyzed friend in hopes of a healing. Unable to approach Jesus through the people, the men went to the roof of the building, where they broke through the tiles and let their friend down in front of Jesus (Luke 5:17-26).

Impressed with this show of faith, Jesus declared that the man's sins were forgiven. Then several scribes and Pharisees accused Jesus of the sin of blasphemy because only God could forgive sin.

Jesus told the critics that His claim to forgive sins was something that no one could prove. But to show that He did have the ability to do that, He would perform a miracle leaving no doubt about His divine power and

P

authority. Jesus ordered the man to stand; when he did, the people were astonished.

PASSION WEEK. See *Holy Week.*

PASSOVER. See *Feast of Passover.*

PAUL THE APOSTLE. A persecutor of the early church who was converted to Christianity after a dramatic encounter with the risen Lord on the road to Damascus (Acts 9:1-6). Paul went on to become the tireless "apostle to the Gentiles" throughout the Mediterranean world.

Through Paul's thirteen epistles in the New Testament, he declared the foundational truth about Jesus that has inspired believers of every generation: God was in Christ, reconciling the world to himself (2 Corinthians 5:19).

PAYING TAXES TO CAESAR. See *Herodians.*

PEACE I GIVE YOU. See *Farewell Address to His Disciples.*

PEACEMAKERS. See *Beatitudes.*

PEARL OF GREAT PRICE. See *Kingdom of God Parables.*

PERSECUTION. See *Farewell Address to His Disciples.*

P

PERSISTENT WIDOW PARABLE. This parable may
have brought a grin to those who first heard it. Jesus told about
a widow—we might call her the woman who wouldn't give up—
who was being treated unfairly by another person. She presented
her case to a local judge, only to be turned away (Luke 18:1-7).

But this woman had a stubborn streak that wouldn't be
denied—she kept pestering the judge to give her justice. Finally,
he gave in and heard her case, not because he was concerned for
her welfare but because her persistence had worn him down.

Jesus applied this parable to the prayer life of kingdom citizens. If an insensitive judge will finally grant justice to a poor
widow, will a loving God not answer the prayers of His own children who pray to Him with persistent faith?

God is never indifferent to our prayers, even though it can
seem that way when we do not receive the answer we want—
or perhaps no answer at all. He may be waiting until we are
spiritually ready to receive His response. Meanwhile, He will
give us grace to handle the situation that brought us to our
knees before Him in the first place. See also *Prayer*.

PETER. Jesus's most prominent disciple, known for his impul-
sive actions and brash personality. Peter swore he would never
deny his Lord, but did exactly that when Jesus was arrested
(Luke 22:54-62). But after being forgiven and restored by Jesus,
he went on to become a bold preacher of the gospel in the early
church in Jerusalem (Acts 2:14-40).

A fisherman from Galilee, Peter became a member of the
Twelve after he was introduced to Jesus by his brother Andrew
(John 1:40-42). Jesus called him Cephas, a name meaning
"stone," perhaps symbolizing what Peter could become in spite
of his shortcomings. His full name was Simon Peter (Matthew
16:16).

Peter was the first of Jesus's disciples to recognize and confess openly that Jesus was the Son of the living God who was on

a divine mission as Savior of the world. Jesus commended Peter for this insight, then promised that His church would be established on those who expressed the same faith that Peter had affirmed (Matthew 16:13-20).

Like many other leaders in the early church, Peter was slow to accept the truth that Jesus was more than the Jewish Messiah. Then God sent a vision that made him realize that Gentiles were also included in God's redemptive plan (Acts 10:1-48). In later years, Peter wrote the epistles of 1 and 2 Peter that are included in the New Testament. He encouraged believers to stand firm in the face of persecution and to deal firmly with heresies that threaten the church.

The apostle Peter shows just how much God can do with a life that is totally committed to Him and His service. See also *Disciples of Jesus.*

PETER'S MOTHER-IN-LAW HEALED. At Peter's house in Capernaum, Jesus found Peter's mother-in-law lying in bed with a fever. Jesus took her by the hand, and she recovered immediately. Her restoration to health was so complete that she got out of bed and began to serve Jesus and her other guests (Mark 1:29-31).

This incident reminds us that even those closest to Jesus are not guaranteed a trouble-free life. But He is the key to victory over our difficulties.

PHARISEE AND TAX COLLECTOR. See *Proud Pharisee Parable.*

PHARISEES. A major religious party of New Testament times known for fastidious observance of the Old Testament law and the oral traditions that had grown up around it. Jesus clashed often with the Pharisees because of their hypocrisy, pride, and extreme legalism.

P

The word *Pharisee* means "separated one." The Pharisees elevated themselves above the common people and took pride in their status as the Jewish officials who devoted their time to the study and interpretation of the law. To them, the rabbinic commentaries and interpretations that had been added to the written law across the centuries were just as important as the original law, handed down by the Lord to Moses. The Pharisees took great offense when Jesus accused them of breaking the commands of God "for the sake of your tradition" (Matthew 15:3).

Jesus was a threat to the Pharisees because He claimed to have religious authority that came directly from God. He criticized them for making a public show of their religious rituals so people would praise them for their piety. This vain, egotistic attitude was just the opposite of the spirit of humility that should characterize citizens of the kingdom of God (Matthew 5:5).

Jesus warned His disciples to avoid what He referred to as "the yeast of the Pharisees" (Luke 12:1)—that is, their hypocrisy. They pretended to be morally superior to others while they were actually corrupt and full of wickedness. See also *Sadducees*; *Woes against the Pharisees*.

PHILIP, DISCIPLE OF JESUS. The member of the Twelve who failed Jesus's test about how to feed the five thousand. In response to the Lord's question on where to buy bread for the crowd in such an isolated place, Philip began to count the financial cost. It didn't dawn on him that Jesus had the power to meet the need through the miraculous multiplication of a few pieces of bread and fish (John 6:5–9).

Philip's lack of understanding was also apparent in Jesus's farewell discourse to His disciples. When He told them He was going away to join God the Father, Philip responded, "Lord, show us the Father" (John 14:8).

Jesus assured Philip and the other disciples that God the Father was standing in their midst. "Anyone who has seen me," He declared, "has seen the Father" (John 14:9).

P

In other encounters with Jesus, Philip fared better. As soon as he became a disciple himself, he brought his friend Bartholomew, also known as Nathanael, to Jesus (John 1:43-46). Philip, along with Andrew, told Jesus about a group of Greeks who wanted to see Him (John 12:20-22). This happened during the Passover celebration in Jerusalem, just a few days before Jesus was put to death. See also *Disciples of Jesus*.

PHILIP, ROMAN RULER. See *Herod*, No. 4.

PICKING GRAIN ON THE SABBATH. See *Sabbath*.

PILATE. The Roman governor of Judea who presided at Jesus's Roman trial. Pilate was convinced that Jesus was innocent of the charges against Him, but eventually caved in to the demands of the Jewish religious leaders and ordered Him to be crucified (Matthew 27:11-26).

Pilate tried to shift blame to Jesus's enemies, literally washing his hands before them in an attempt to avoid responsibility. Pilate is a good example of people in high positions who give in to public opinion rather than do what is right. See also *Trials of Jesus*.

PONTIUS PILATE. See *Pilate*.

POOL OF BETHESDA. A spring-fed pool in the city of Jerusalem where Jesus healed a lame man who had been disabled for thirty-eight years (John 5:1-8).

Archaeologists have discovered a pool in the old city of Jerusalem that may be the very site where this miracle occurred. This excavated fountain was covered by five arches, echoing the biblical description that the pool of Bethesda was "surrounded by five covered colonnades" (verse 2). See also *Lame Man Healed on the Sabbath*.

POOL OF SILOAM. A water reservoir in Jerusalem where a blind man washed and had his sight restored, in response to the command of Jesus (John 9:1–11).

This pool was also known as Hezekiah's Pool. The reservoir and an adjoining tunnel were built by King Hezekiah of Judah about seven centuries before Jesus's time. Water flowed into the pool from a spring outside the walls of Jerusalem. The king had the reservoir constructed to provide water for the city in the event of a prolonged siege by the Assyrian army (2 Kings 20:20). See also *Man Born Blind Healed*.

POOR IN SPIRIT. See *Beatitudes*.

POSSESSIONS. Jesus had a lot to say about earthly possessions. In one of His parables, He cautioned against greed, the insatiable desire for more material things that could blind a person to more important spiritual realities (Luke 12:13–21).

Jesus also used His encounter with a wealthy young man to teach His disciples a valuable lesson about the attraction of great riches. This man turned away from following Jesus, from becoming a citizen of the kingdom of God, because he could not give up his riches (Mark 10:17–23).

In His Sermon on the Mount, Jesus cautioned His disciples, "You cannot serve both God and money" (Matthew 6:24; *mammon:* KJV). He was saying that it's impossible to serve God and the things of this world at the same time. Putting God first will keep possessions from becoming the main concern of our lives. See also *Rich Fool Parable; Rich Young Ruler; Treasures in Heaven*.

POUNDS PARABLE. See *Minas Parable.*

PRAYER. Communion with God, something that Jesus enjoyed constantly as He sought His Father's will and drew strength from His presence. Not only did Jesus pray personally (Luke 6:12), but He also taught His disciples how they should pray through the Lord's Prayer (Matthew 6:9-13).

Jesus emphasized that genuine prayer does not consist of mouthing pious phrases to impress others, but rather communing with God in private meditation. He also declared that persistence in prayer is important (Luke 18:1-8). Constant and consistent communion with God shows that prayer is a priority in Christians' lives and that they have faith in the loving Father who has promised to answer prayers.

Jesus also taught His followers to pray for others, especially the people who have mistreated them. Putting

PROMISES OF JESUS

Ask, and You Will Receive

Beatitudes

Consider the Lilies

Farewell Address to His Disciples

Find One's Life by Losing It

Firstborn from Among the Dead

Great Commission

Holy Spirit

Humble Will Be Exalted

Kingdom of God

Remain in Me

Yoke Is Easy

P

the matter in God's hands through earnest prayer can help Christians overcome the urge to hate others and return wrong for wrong (Luke 6:27-36). See also *Lord's Prayer; Persistent Widow Parable.*

PRECIOUS PEARL. See *Kingdom of God Parables.*

PREEXISTENCE OF JESUS. The doctrine that Jesus existed with God the Father long before He was born in human form into the world. This truth was best expressed by the apostle John in the very beginning of his gospel: "In the beginning was the Word, and the Word was with God, and the Word was God. He was with God in the beginning" (John 1:1-2).

Notice that the first three words of this verse match the first three words of the Bible, "In the beginning" (Genesis 1:1). Just as God existed before time began with the creation, so Jesus existed with God the Father as the eternal Word.

When He was born to Mary and Joseph in Bethlehem, Jesus took on human flesh at a definite time and place. As John expressed it, "The Word became flesh and made his dwelling among us" (John 1:14). Jesus's mission was to identify with humankind and become God's agent of redemption in a fallen world. See also *Fullness of Time.*

PRESENTATION OF JESUS IN THE TEMPLE. Forty days after Jesus was born, His parents dedicated Him in the temple in Jerusalem. During this ceremony, they presented an offering as a purification ritual. It was a token of the consecration to God of their firstborn son (Luke 2:21-24).

Mary and Joseph's offering on this occasion consisted of two doves and two young pigeons rather than a lamb. This indicated the humble circumstances of the home into which Jesus was born. See also *Anna; Simeon.*

PRIEST. See *Offices of Christ.*

PRINCE OF THIS WORLD. See *Satan.*

PRODIGAL SON PARABLE. This is probably the best known and most popular parable from the lips of Jesus (Luke 15:11-32). The essentials of the account are well known.

The younger of two sons convinced his father to give him his share of the estate in advance, then set out to see the world. As this son celebrated his new-found freedom, it didn't take him long to squander his money through wild living. He wound up the destitute servant of a Gentile landowner. The young man became almost hungry enough to eat the food he was doling out to his employer's pigs.

But then this young man "came to his senses" (verse 17) and decided to return home. He determined to throw himself on his father's mercy, asking to become a hired servant rather than to be accepted back as a privileged son. But his father ran out to meet him, embraced him warmly, and threw a homecoming party in his honor. "Let's have a feast and celebrate," he declared. "For this son of mine was dead and is alive again; he was lost and is found" (verses 23-24).

This father's attitude of love and acceptance was exactly the opposite of that of his older son—the wayward son's brother. The elder brother, proud of his record as an obedient son, refused to take part in the homecoming festivities. He resented all the attention being showered on his younger brother.

This spiteful attitude symbolized the attitude of the Pharisees. Their pride and self-righteousness kept them from enjoying the riches of God's grace and acceptance. They were as far away from God as the prodigal son had been in his state of rebellion. But unlike him, they would remain lost—unless they threw themselves on the mercy of the Lord.

RELATIVES OF JESUS

Brothers of Jesus

Elizabeth

Genealogies of Jesus

James, Half Brother of Jesus

John the Baptist

Joseph, Husband of Mary

Judas, Half Brother of Jesus

Mary, Mother of Jesus

Zechariah

PRODUCES A COIN FOR THE TEMPLE TAX.
All adult Jewish males in Jesus's time were required to pay a tax for the maintenance and operation of the temple in Jerusalem. One day a temple official asked Peter if Jesus paid this mandatory tax. This question may have been an attempt to discredit Jesus for failing to meet His obligations as a Jewish citizen.

When Peter brought the matter to Jesus, He agreed this was a requirement that He should satisfy. So He sent Peter to the nearby Sea of Galilee to catch a fish, predicting this fish would contain a coin that could be used to pay the tax for both himself and Peter (Matthew 17:24-27).

This miracle has been debated for centuries by Bible interpreters. Was Jesus guilty of using His miraculous powers to meet His own needs—something He refused to do when He was tempted by Satan in the wilderness (Luke 4:1-13)? Is this passage an allegory that Matthew included in his gospel to show the all-knowing power of Jesus?

After all, He did predict that the first fish Peter caught would contain the needed coin.

Some interpreters believe that what Jesus actually told Peter to do was to return to his job as a fisherman long enough to earn the money to pay the required tax. The problem with this theory is that Jesus told Peter to "throw out your line" (verse 27), not the net that Peter used in his vocation as a commercial fisherman.

Without a satisfactory answer to these questions, we have no choice but to accept the miracle at face value. Ultimately, aren't all His miracles clothed in mystery? We accept their reality because Jesus was the all-powerful and all-knowing Son of God.

PROPHET. See *Offices of Christ.*

PROPHET WITHOUT HONOR. See *Nazareth.*

PROUD PHARISEE PARABLE. Jesus told this parable to correct the attitude of those who boasted about their own righteousness while condemning the shortcomings of others. He deliberately chose a Pharisee and a tax collector—two men who represented the extremes of Jewish life—to drive home His point (Luke 18:9–14).

The Pharisee observed every detail of the Old Testament law. But the tax collector—a despised pawn of the Roman government—cared little for the law's rituals and regulations. Both men prayed in the temple, but their prayers were poles apart.

As he prayed, the Pharisee focused a critical eye on the tax collector, thanking the Lord that he was not like the other man. The Pharisee also boasted that he fasted twice a week and gave a tenth of His income to religious causes. His excessive zeal probably grew out of his belief that God's acceptance depended on his own good works.

The tax collector did not pretend to have a long list of good works to present to God. Out of a sense of unworthiness, he admitted he was a sinner, throwing himself on God's mercy.

Jesus declared that the tax collector rather than the Pharisee was justified in God's sight. Honest confession of sin and sincere repentance are the only things that matter in the eyes of the Lord.

PUBLICAN. See *Tax Collector.*

PURE IN HEART. See *Beatitudes.*

QUIRINIUS. A Roman official cited by the gospel of Luke as governor of the province of Syria when Jesus was born (Luke 2:2; Cyrenius: KJV).

For a time, some scholars questioned Luke's accuracy on this point, since secular history showed that another Roman official ruled over Syria when Jesus was born. But the discovery of an ancient inscription has proved that Quirinius served in Syria at two different times with two distinct responsibilities. It was probably during his first term of service as a senior military officer that Jesus was born.

RABBI. A title of honor for a Jewish teacher of the law in New Testament times; the term means "teacher." In John's gospel, several different people addressed Jesus by using this title (John 1:38, 49; 3:2, 4:31; 6:25). See also *Authority of Jesus.*

RAISES THE DEAD. See *Jairus's Daughter Raised from the Dead; Lazarus Raised from the Dead; Widow's Son Raised from the Dead.*

READINESS FOR JESUS'S RETURN. See *Second Coming.*

REDEEMER. The prophet Isaiah's prophetic title for Jesus, declaring that He would free people from their bondage to sin and death (Isaiah 59:20).

In Old Testament times, a kinsman-redeemer was a person who stepped forward to help a member of the family who had suffered some misfortune, such as losing his property because of crushing debt. Isaiah used this imagery to show that the future Messiah would rescue people from their spiritual darkness.

Jesus fulfilled this prediction when He gave His life as humanity's redeemer. Trapped by sin, people have no way of escape from their hopeless condition except through the atoning death of Jesus Christ.

REMAIN IN ME. A phrase of Jesus which encourages believers to stay in constant contact with Him—the source of their strength and their hope of eternal life. He used the phrase several times in John 15:4–10 (*abide in me*: KJV), part of His long farewell discourse to His disciples in chapters 14–17 of John's gospel.

To remain in Jesus means to stay connected to Him through prayer, quiet devotional times, Bible study, meditation on His teachings, and ministry to others in His name. He has promised to those who remain in Him that He will remain in them, giving strength to live joyous and victorious lives. See also *True Vine.*

RENDER TO CAESAR WHAT IS CAESAR'S. See *Herodians.*

REPENTANCE. See *Atonement; Baptism of Jesus; Mediator.*

RESURRECTED FROM THE GRAVE. Jesus's most spectacular miracle was coming back to life after His death and burial. He told His disciples several times that this would happen (Matthew 16:21; Luke 9:21-22, 43-45; 18:31-34), but they never seemed to grasp the reality of this event until Jesus appeared to them several times in His post-resurrection body.

All four gospels record the resurrection, but differ in some of the details they include. For example, they mention several different groups of women who visited the tomb on Sunday morning (Matthew 28:1; Mark 16:1; Luke 24:1; John 20:1). The Gospels also provide differing details on the angels who appeared at the tomb and the way they greeted these women (Matthew 28:2-3; Mark 16:4-5; Luke 24:4).

But the Gospels agree on the most important fact—that the tomb was open and Jesus's body was gone. As two angels told the women, "Why do you look for the living among the dead? He is not here; he has risen!" (Luke 24:5-6).

Some people wonder about Jesus's statement to the disciples that He would be raised "on the third day" (Luke 9:22). Actually, He was in the grave only about thirty-two hours—from mid-afternoon on Friday until sometime before dawn on Sunday morning—one full day plus parts of two other days. But the Jews referred to a partial day as if it were a full day, so Jesus was resurrected on the third day, just as He predicted.

RETALIATION. See *Eye for Eye.*

RICH FOOL PARABLE. While Jesus was teaching a crowd, one man interrupted Him with an unusual request. The man wanted Jesus to confront his brother and order him to share his family inheritance. This showed the man was more concerned with earthly possession than he was about the spiritual truths coming from the lips of Jesus (Luke 12:13-21).

Jesus responded by telling about a wealthy farmer whose main goal in life was accumulating earthly goods. When his crops yielded a bountiful harvest, he tore down his old barns and built bigger ones to hold the surplus.

Then, God himself appeared to the farmer and pointed out the foolishness of his self-centered ways. In the parable, God told the man that he would die that night, and other people would enjoy the goods he had worked so hard to accumulate.

Jesus summed it up like this: "Life does not consist in an abundance of possessions" (verse 15). It is better to seek the Lord's blessing than to heap up earthly riches. What a person does for the cause of the kingdom of God can never be taken away by time, death, or the circumstances of life. See also *Possessions*; *Treasures in Heaven*.

RICH MAN AND LAZARUS PARABLE.

This parable exemplifies one of Jesus's favorite teaching techniques—turning things

THE SABBATH AND JESUS

Demons and Demon Possession, No. 7

Expert in the Law

Lame Man Healed on the Sabbath

Man with Body Fluid Healed

Man with Deformed Hand Healed

Sabbath

around to show that the truth may be the exact opposite of what people think.

Jesus told about a rich man who enjoyed all the finer things of life, including luxurious clothes and food. Outside the gate of his expensive house a poor man named Lazarus stationed himself every day to forage for the scraps of food that the rich man's household servants threw out. The rich man showed no concern for Lazarus or anyone else. He was totally self-centered and cared nothing for the spiritual values of God's kingdom (Luke 16:19–31).

Both men died at about the same time, but they went to separate places in the afterlife. Lazarus was received to Abraham's side—a symbol of heaven. The rich man wound up in hades—the shadowy underworld that was known as the abode of the dead.

Now the situation was exactly the opposite of what the two had experienced on earth. Lazarus was comfortable and content, but the rich man begged Lazarus to cool his tongue with a finger dipped in water. But they were separated by a chasm that neither could cross.

Jesus was warning about the grave consequences of the decisions we make in this life. A life devoted to material things, lived for oneself while ignoring the needs of others, will result in eternal separation from God.

RICH MAN'S TOMB. See *Joseph of Arimathea.*

RICH YOUNG RULER. A man who turned away from following Jesus because his riches stood in the way of his total commitment (Mark 10:17–31). The man had every comfort the earth could provide, but sensed that something was missing from his life. So he asked Jesus, "What must I do to inherit eternal life?" (verse 17).

Jesus replied by quoting several of the Ten Commandments, suggesting that observing these laws was one key to what the young man was searching for. The man insisted that he had followed these laws from an early age.

Jesus immediately realized what this person needed. Although the man had kept these important laws, he didn't know the meaning of sacrificing for a higher spiritual good. To experience life in all its fullness, both now and forever, the young man needed to give up what he valued most in life—his earthly riches. But he could not do that, so he walked away with a sad expression.

Jesus explained to His disciples that wealth is a dangerous thing. It can actually prevent people from entering the kingdom of God. This happens when they place their faith in material things rather than God's promise to provide for their needs. See also *Treasures in Heaven*.

ROAD TO DAMASCUS. See *Paul the Apostle.*

ROMAN EMPIRE. The pagan government that dominated the ancient world—including the nation of Israel—during New Testament times. The Romans ruled their Jewish subjects through appointed local officials such as Herod the Great and Pontius Pilate. Jesus was executed on the false charge that He claimed to be king of the Jews in opposition to the authority of Rome (John 19:12-16). See also *Caesar Augustus.*

ROOSTER CROWS. See *Lord's Supper.*

ROYAL OFFICIAL'S SON HEALED. Jesus was at Cana, a village in Galilee, when He was approached by a royal official. This man was probably a servant or advisor of Herod Antipas, Roman ruler over the province of Galilee. The man begged Jesus to come to Capernaum, a city about twenty miles away, and heal his gravely ill son (John 4:46-53).

Jesus did not follow this desperate man, instead sending him to his house with the assurance that his son would recover.

The official took Jesus at His word and set out for Capernaum. Before the man reached his house, servants met him with the news that his son had made a miraculous recovery. Jesus had healed the boy without leaving Cana.

This miracle shows that Jesus is master over space and time. He had the supernatural ability to heal this child from twenty miles away. John's gospel includes this event as one of the signs of God's power at work through His Son, Jesus Christ.

SABBATH. The seventh day of the week, or Saturday—a time set aside for worship and rest by the Jewish people. The Old Testament law specified that this sacred day should be observed by stopping all work (Exodus 20:10), just as God rested on the seventh day following the six days of creation (Genesis 2:3).

The Pharisees often criticized Jesus for healing people on the Sabbath. To them, this was a flagrant violation of the law. But Jesus pointed out that delivering people from their hopeless condition was more important than following a restrictive rule (Matthew 12:11-12).

On one occasion the Pharisees condemned Jesus and His disciples for picking a few grains of wheat or barley on the Sabbath to satisfy their hunger (Matthew 12:1-8). Jesus referred the Pharisees to a situation in the Old Testament in which David and his warriors were starving because they were being chased by King Saul. They entered the tabernacle and ate loaves of sacred bread, which only the priests were supposed to eat (1 Samuel 21:1-6).

To Jesus this meant that human need was more important than the law's legalistic requirements. He told the Pharisees that "the Sabbath was made for man, not man for the Sabbath" (Mark 2:27).

In His attitude toward the Sabbath, Jesus went even farther than this enlightened interpretation. As the Son of God, with unlimited authority, He was actually the "Lord of the Sabbath" (Matthew 12:8), above the law itself. This was one of Jesus's statements that led His enemies to charge Him with blasphemy. See also *Lord's Day*.

SADDUCEES. Prosperous and influential members of a priestly party that opposed Jesus and His teachings. On one occasion they tried to trap Him with a question about the afterlife. The Sadducees did not believe in a bodily resurrection; they hoped to make Jesus look ridiculous with whatever answer He gave to their hypothetical question (Luke 20:27-40).

What, they asked Jesus, about a woman who was widowed seven times after marriage to seven different brothers? Which man's wife would she be in the afterlife? Basically, the Sadducees were saying that the doctrine of the bodily resurrection was unreasonable.

Jesus replied that His questioners were judging heavenly matters with earthly logic. Relationships in heaven would be different than those that existed on earth. He went on to declare that the Lord had declared, centuries earlier, "I am . . . the God of Abraham, the God of Isaac and the God of Jacob" (Exodus 3:6). Jesus emphasized that God had not said, "I *was*" but "I *am*." These three patriarchs had been dead for many years when the Lord made this statement.

On the basis of this affirmation from the Lord himself, Jesus declared that God "is not the God of the dead, but of the living" (Luke 20:38). So bodily resurrection and existence in the afterlife are assured. See also *Pharisees*.

SALIM. See *Aenon*.

SALOME. One of the women who looked on as Jesus was crucified and who brought spices to the tomb to anoint His body on resurrection morning (Mark 15:40; 16:1).

Salome may be the same person identified by Matthew's gospel as "the mother of Zebedee's sons" (Matthew 27:56), or the disciples James and John, who were the sons of a man named Zebedee. If so, she would be the woman who asked Jesus to give her sons positions of leadership in His kingdom (Matthew 20:20–21). Whether she was thinking of this kingdom in earthly or spiritual terms, she was a typical mother who wanted the best for her boys.

Jesus set the record straight by reminding this mother and her sons that kingdom citizens must drink the cup of suffering that belongs to those who follow Him. See also *Women at the Cross and Tomb*.

SALT OF THE EARTH. A phrase from Jesus's Sermon on the Mount that challenges believers to exercise their positive influence in a godless society (Matthew 5:13).

In New Testament times, long before refrigeration, salt was used as a meat preservative. It was also added to bland food to make it taste better. By using this imagery, Jesus taught His disciples to demonstrate their distinctive purity and holiness before others. The inner joy they experienced as citizens of God's kingdom might cause others to seek the Savior they served.

SALVATION. See *Light of the World*; *True Vine*.

SAMARIA. One of three distinct regions of Palestine during New Testament times. The others were Judea in the south and Galilee in the north. Samaria was sandwiched between these two territories.

Most Jews of Jesus's time had nothing to do with the inhabitants of Samaria. Jews generally considered the Samaritans lowlifes, people who had corrupted their Jewish bloodline by intermarrying with foreigners in the distant past. This prejudice among the Jews was so deep that when they traveled the length of Palestine they detoured around the region of Samaria.

But Jesus accepted Samaritans and treated them kindly. No one was beyond the reach of His love and grace. See also *Good Samaritan Parable*; *Woman at the Well*.

SANHEDRIN. The Jewish high court in Jerusalem that convicted Jesus of blasphemy for claiming to perform the works of God. The high priest of Israel presided over this body of seventy religious leaders (Matthew 26:57–59; *council:* KJV).

The Sanhedrin had jurisdiction over Jewish religious matters, but it did not have the authority to condemn an offender to death. This is why the group delivered Jesus to Pilate, the Roman governor, with the recommendation that He be executed for crimes against the Roman government (Matthew 27:2–24). See also *Trials of Jesus*.

SATAN. An evil being who opposed Jesus and tried to convince Him to turn aside from the divine mission on which He had been sent. This occurred at the beginning of Jesus's public ministry as He was tempted by Satan in the wilderness (Luke 4:1–13).

Jesus showed His power over Satan by refusing to fall victim to these temptations. He also released people from Satan's power by casting out the demons with which Satan had afflicted their lives.

The apostle John saw Jesus's entire ministry as a mission to "destroy the devil's work" (1 John 3:8). The apostle Paul declared that Jesus's atoning death was a victory over Satan and his demonic hosts (Colossians 2:15).

In the Gospels, another name for Satan is Beelzebul (Matthew 12:24). Jesus also referred to him as the "evil one" (Matthew 13:19; *wicked one:* KJV) and the "prince of this world" (John 12:31).

In the book of Revelation, the apostle John predicted that Jesus Christ will eventually triumph over all evil forces at the end of the age. Satan and his evil henchman known as the false prophet will be cast into a lake of fire (Revelation 19:20). See also *Temptations of Jesus*.

SCRIBE. See *Expert in the Law.*

SEA OF GALILEE.

A body of water fed by the Jordan River. On this beautiful little lake, several of Jesus's disciples fished for a living. He called two sets of brothers—Peter and Andrew and James and John—away from their fishing nets on these waters to follow Him and become "fishers of men" (Mark 1:17 KJV). These seasoned commercial fishermen were particularly impressed with Jesus when He produced a huge catch of fish in broad daylight, after they had fished all night and caught nothing (Luke 5:1-11).

This body of water is actually not a sea but a freshwater lake about fourteen miles long by seven miles wide at its broadest point. Its emerald blue waters are usually calm, but sudden storms

SALVATION IN JESUS

Bright Morning Star

"I Am" Statements of Jesus, No. 3

Light of the World

Mediator

Messiah

Seven Sayings from the Cross, No. 5

True Vine

Wedding Banquet Parable

can turn it into a raging torrent. This is what happened to Jesus and His disciples on one occasion when they were crossing the lake in a small fishing boat. He calmed the waters with a simple command to the wind and waves: "Quiet! Be still!" (Mark 4:39).

Jesus spent much of His ministry in the area known as Galilee, which took its name from the lake. On the shore were several towns that He visited during His Galilean ministry—Bethsaida, Capernaum, Chorazin, and Magadan. Two other names for this lake that appear in the Gospels are the Lake of Gennesaret (Luke 5:1) and the Sea of Tiberias (John 6:1). See also *Galilee*.

SEA OF TIBERIAS. See *Sea of Galilee*.

SECOND COMING. The doctrine that Jesus will return to the earth in glory at the end of the present age. Jesus foretold this event to His disciples on the night before He was crucified (John 14:3). In later years, the apostle Paul assured believers of the certainty of this happening (1 Corinthians 15:23; Colossians 3:4).

Jesus instructed His disciples to "keep your lamps burning" (Luke 12:35), or always to be ready for His return. He also used the analogy of a burglar breaking into a house at night to show the second coming could happen at a time when it was least expected (Luke 12:38-48).

Jesus's unexpected return is also the theme of His parable about ten virgins who were attending a wedding (Matthew 25:1-13). During the night, holding their oil-burning lamps, they waited for the arrival of the bridegroom. Five of these women had brought plenty of oil for their lamps. But five did not, and their lamps ran out of oil at the very moment when the bridegroom appeared. Jesus drove home His point with the declaration, "Therefore keep watch, because you do not know the day or the hour" (verse 13).

Jesus also declared that His second coming would involve judgment. He would separate the righteous from the unrighteous like a shepherd separates the sheep from the goats in his flock. The righteous—those who have committed their lives to Jesus and who show His love toward others—will enjoy everlasting fellowship with God. But the unrighteous—those who have rejected Jesus and show no concern for others—will be consigned to eternal separation from God. Jesus made it clear that He considered our deeds of kindness to others just the same as ministry to Him (Matthew 25:31-46). See also *Noah*; *Olivet Discourse*.

SEEK FIRST THE KINGDOM OF GOD. See *Kingdom of God*.

SENDS OUT HIS FOLLOWERS. Jesus sent His twelve original disciples, as well as a group of seventy-two other followers, throughout the countryside in teams of two to teach and heal. This tour would provide valuable training for these believers, as well as expand the reach of Jesus's ministry beyond what He could accomplish on His own (Matthew 10:1-42; Mark 6:7; Luke 10:1-24).

Before these people set out, Jesus gave them explicit instructions: They should travel lightly and not waste time by exchanging elaborate greetings with their audience. If they were rejected, they should move on quickly to other people who would be more receptive to their message.

Jesus knew the attitude with which these disciples went was also important. He cautioned them to be "as shrewd as snakes and as innocent as doves" (Matthew 10:16)—that is, clever enough to secure a hearing for the gospel but kind and respectful toward their audience at the same time.

The preaching mission of the Twelve was meant to announce the nearness of the kingdom of God in the person of Jesus, while the seventy-two were charged with a broader missionary purpose. They symbolized the future time when Jesus's followers would be sent out to preach the gospel to all nations—perhaps a New Testament allusion to the numerous Gentile nations listed in the first book of the Old Testament (Genesis 10:1-32). See also *Acts of the Apostles*; *Great Commission*.

SERMON ON THE MOUNT. Jesus's long speech to His followers, describing how they should live as citizens of the kingdom of God. Matthew's account of these teachings (chapters 5-7) is the most familiar, but a shorter version also appears in the gospel of Luke (6:17-49). Here's a brief summary of the ten major principles in this teaching, as presented in Matthew's gospel.

1. **Christian influence** (5:13-16). As salt and light, believers are expected to exercise their influence for good in a pagan society. Through their words and actions, Christians show God's love to others, leading people to the divine light that illuminates believers' lives. Jesus told His followers not to put their light "under a bushel" (verse 15 KJV). They should live out their faith with boldness as righteous witnesses in a sinful world.

2. **Authentic righteousness** (5:17-47). Genuine righteousness issues from the heart. Kingdom citizens will avoid swearing and oath taking, will guard their hearts against anger and sexual lust, and will express love for their enemies.

3. **Motive does matter** (6:1-18). Good deeds such as praying, giving, and fasting should not be performed to impress others. The only right motives for such actions are genuine love and compassion.

4. **Setting priorities** (6:19-34). Believers should put following Jesus ahead of everything else in life. This will free them from undue anxiety over earthly concerns.

5. **Judging belongs to God** (7:1-6). Kingdom citizens should not judge people in a harsh and thoughtless manner. Jesus declared this would be like a person with a plank (*beam*: KJV) in his eye trying to remove a tiny splinter (*mote*: KJV) from the eye of another. Only God has the wisdom to stand in judgment over others.

6. **Persistence in prayer** (7:7-12). Believers should claim the privileges and blessings of prayer by asking, seeking, and

knocking—laying their concerns persistently before their heavenly Father. They are assured He will give them what they need when they pray in the right attitude and in accordance with His will.

7. **Making good choices** (7:13-14). The way to God is not the broad and easy path that most people follow as the course of least resistance. We should approach Him through the narrow way of self-discipline and submission to His will.

8. **Known by deeds** (7:15-20). Believers are judged by their deeds or actions, just as a tree is known for the fruit it bears. Citizens of the kingdom of God may be recognized as those who perform works of righteousness to the glory of God the Father.

9. **An exclusive kingdom** (7:21-23). Jesus declared that not all people who claim to follow Him will enter the kingdom of God. These people are full of talk but no substance. His kingdom is reserved for those who obey God and devote their lives to doing His will.

10. **A firm foundation** (7:24-27). Jesus ended His Sermon on the Mount with a parable about two builders. One built his house on sandy soil, but the other built on solid rock. The second house withstood the storm, but the one on the unstable sand collapsed. The message of this parable is that people who plant their lives on Jesus and His teachings will be able to ride out every storm of life. See also *Beatitudes*.

SERVANT, JESUS AS. See *Isaiah*; *Washes the Disciples' Feet*.

SEVEN SAYINGS FROM THE CROSS. In His final hours, while suffering on the cross, Jesus uttered seven sayings that reveal His character and define His mission as the Savior of the world.

Three of these sayings were recorded by Luke, three by John, and one—a quotation from the Old Testament—occurs in both

Matthew and Mark. Thus, all four gospels are needed to give us a complete record of Jesus's final words.

1. **"Father, forgive them, for they do not know what they are doing"** (Luke 23:34). Jesus had taught His followers to be quick to forgive—to harbor no resentment or malice toward those who did them harm. To the jeering crowd around the cross, this prayer was a flesh-and-blood demonstration of this principle.

2. **"Truly I tell you, today you will be with me in paradise"** (Luke 23:43). Jesus spoke these words to a criminal on the cross next to Him. This man had asked to be remembered in Jesus's future kingdom. The request implied that the man believed in Jesus and repented of his sin. Jesus forgave the man and assured him that he didn't have to wait to enter the kingdom. He would enjoy fellowship with Jesus in heaven immediately.

3. **"Woman, here is your son. . . . Here is your mother"** (John 19:26-27). With these words, Jesus made sure His mother, Mary, would be taken care of after His death, by the disciple John. Jesus had several half-brothers, Mary's other sons, so why did He need to designate John as her caretaker? Jesus knew at this point that His brothers were skeptical toward Him and His ministry. But John had spent three years with Jesus as a believer. He could provide comfort to Mary by recalling memories of their time together.

4. **"I am thirsty"** (John 19:28). The irony of these three simple words is that the One who offered the water of life now felt famished because of exposure to the elements and loss of body fluid. Jesus was completely human, so He craved water like any other person. As He poured himself out completely for others, His suffering was real.

5. **"My God, my God, why have you forsaken me?"** (Matthew 27:46; Mark 15:34). These words, known as the cry of dereliction, are a quotation from an Old Testament writer who felt abandoned by the Lord (Psalm 22:1). This must have been Jesus's way of expressing the feeling of emptiness and loneliness brought on by His intense suffering. At this moment, the One

who knew no sin took the sins of the whole world upon himself (2 Corinthians 5:21). His cry of anguish reflects the separation from God that sin always creates in the human heart.
The Aramaic form of this phrase—*Eli, Eli, lama sabachthani* (KJV)—also appears in both Matthew and Mark's account.

6. **"It is finished"** (John 19:30). These words were not a sigh but a shout—a firm declaration by the Messiah that He had completed the mission for which He had been sent into the world. The climactic event in God's redemptive plan was Jesus's death on the cross.

7. **"Father, into your hands I commit my spirit"** (Luke 23:46). These words serve as both a summary of and a conclusion to Jesus's earthly ministry. He was born of God's Spirit and anointed for ministry by the Spirit, and He taught and healed through the Spirit's power. Now Jesus committed His Spirit into the Father's hands, yielding His life voluntarily as an atoning sacrifice for sinful humanity.

SEVEN SIGNS OF JOHN'S GOSPEL. A sign is something that points to a meaning beyond an event itself. John's gospel is unique among the others in that it separates out seven miracles that Jesus performed, suggesting that each had a deeper meaning. Following is a list of John's seven signs, along with a summary of the possible meaning of each.

1. **Turns water into wine** (John 2:1–11). Jesus produced an abundance of wine from six large jars of water, each holding about thirty gallons. This was many times more than was needed for guests at this wedding and points to Jesus's ability to provide abundantly for every need.

2. **Heals a royal official's son** (John 4:46-54). Though He was several miles away, Jesus healed this boy at the home of a royal official. This sign declares that Jesus has the power to accomplish good anywhere at any time. Through prayer, we can call on Him for comfort and strength in any situation.

3. **Heals a paralyzed man** (John 5:1-9). This healing highlights the compassion of Jesus for a helpless invalid and the man's instant obedience to the Lord's command. The man's restoration to health is a perfect picture of our hopeless condition as sinners and Jesus's forgiveness when we turn to Him in faith and repentance.

4. **Feeds five thousand people** (John 6:5-13). Jesus multiplied a boy's lunch of five small loaves of bread and two small fish to feed a hungry crowd. He could have created these provisions from nothing but chose to use what the boy gave willingly. Jesus wants His followers today to present Him with the little they have to offer. In His hands, Christians' tiny gifts of time, money, and service can grow into blessings for many people.

5. **Walks on the water** (John 6:15-21). The disciples were alone in a boat on the Sea of Galilee when they were overwhelmed by a sudden storm. Suddenly Jesus appeared, walking toward them on the water. He calmed their fears and joined them in the boat. Then they realized they had not been alone after all—Jesus had been watching them from a distant hillside where He was praying. This miracle tells us that Jesus is always near His followers, even in their moments of fear and uncertainty. Christians are never out of range of His voice saying, "It is I; don't be afraid" (verse 20).

6. **Heals a man born blind** (John 9:1-41). This miracle contrasts the newfound sight of a man born blind with the spiritual blindness of the self-righteous Pharisees. The blind man believed in Jesus, so his sight was restored. But the Pharisees, refusing to believe, remained in their blindness. So this miraculous sign warns us against the worst kind of spiritual darkness—that caused by doubt and unbelief.

7. **Raises Lazarus from the dead** (John 11:38-44). This narrative of the raising of Lazarus is different from the two other miraculous restorations from the dead recorded in the Gospels—Jairus's daughter (Matthew 9:18-26) and a widow's son (Luke 7:11-17). Only in the Lazarus narrative did Jesus raise someone who had been dead for four days. And only here did He proclaim himself to be

the "resurrection and the life" (John 11:25). Thus, the meaning of this miracle is that Jesus is victorious—without any doubt—over death and the grave. He promises bodily resurrection and eternal life to those who place their faith in Him.

SEVENTY SENT OUT. See *Sends Out His Followers.*

SHEEP AND GOATS. See *Second Coming.*

SHREWD MANAGER PARABLE. Jesus told about a hired servant who managed a rich landowner's property (Luke 16:1-12). This servant was suspected of mismanagement, so the landowner served notice that he was under investigation, telling him to turn over the records of all his business transactions.

The quick-thinking manager came up with a scheme to protect himself: he called in his employer's debtors one by one and reduced the amount they owed, hoping they would return these favors and come to his aid in case he was fired.

The landowner actually praised his servant for this shrewd action. It may have been a backhanded compliment like, "I didn't realize what a clever and scheming scoundrel he is."

Some people wonder why Jesus would tell a parable that seems to commend a schemer for his dishonesty. But Jesus did not compliment this manager; his employer did. Then Jesus drove home the parable's message: "The people of this world are more shrewd in dealing with their own kind than are the people of the light" (verse 8).

Just as this manager showed foresight in planning for the future, so should Jesus's followers. This applies especially to the life to come—people should make sure they are prepared for the eternity that follows their earthly existence. See also *Second Coming.*

SIGN OF JONAH. Even miracles did not convince the Pharisees that Jesus was the divine Son of God. When they asked for a more spectacular sign as proof of His messiahship, He told them the only sign they would be shown was the sign of Jonah (Luke 11:29-32).

Just as the prophet Jonah was delivered from the stomach of a great fish (Jonah 2:10), so Jesus would be resurrected from the dead at some future time. This would be a dramatic sign that no one could deny. See also *Resurrected from the Grave.*

S

SILOAM. See *Pool of Siloam.*

SIMEON. A devout and elderly man who blessed the baby Jesus when He was presented at the temple in Jerusalem (Luke 2:21-35).

Simeon had been waiting expectantly for the Messiah's coming. He happened to be in the temple at the very moment that Mary and Joseph brought their baby in to present Him before the Lord. Through the inspiration of the Holy Spirit, Simeon recognized immediately that this child was the long-awaited Savior.

In a prayer that became known as the Nunc Dimittis, Simeon recognized that this child was destined to become the glory of the people of Israel as well as a light to the Gentile world—a universal Savior.

But Simeon went on to deliver sad news for Jesus's mother, Mary, predicting that a sword would pierce her heart. She did not understand the words at the time. But the day would come when Mary would experience their reality as she saw her firstborn Son nailed to a cross.

SIMON OF CYRENE. A bystander who was pressed into service by Roman soldiers to carry Jesus's cross to the crucifixion site (Matthew 27:32). The gospel of Mark adds the detail that Simon was the father of Alexander and Rufus (Mark 15:21). This Rufus may be the same believer to whom the apostle Paul later sent greetings (Romans 16:13).

Cyrene was the capital city of a Roman district in northern Africa. Simon may have been a Greek-speaking Jew visiting Jerusalem to observe the Passover when Jesus was crucified.

SIMON PETER. See *Peter.*

SIMON THE PHARISEE. A prominent Pharisee who invited Jesus to a meal in his home. When a sinful woman poured perfume on His feet and dried them with her hair, Jesus used the occasion to teach Simon about generosity and forgiveness (Luke 7:36-50).

Jesus condemned the Pharisees as a group because of their legalistic traditions and self-righteous attitudes. But His acceptance of Simon's invitation shows that He did not exclude all Pharisees from His ministry. Jesus also patiently explained the new birth to a Pharisee named Nicodemus (John 3:1-21). And a Pharisee known as Joseph was a secret follower who claimed Jesus's body and gave Him a decent burial (John 19:38-40). See also *Anointing of Jesus.*

SIMON THE ZEALOT. A disciple of Jesus who may have belonged to a radical Jewish sect known as the Zealots. Members of this group were known for their fanatical opposition to the Romans who ruled over the Jews.

Simon is mentioned in all three lists of the disciples that appear in the Gospels (Matthew 10:4; Mark 3:18; Luke 6:15). In the book of Acts, after Jesus's ascension, Simon is mentioned with the other eleven disciples as they prayed together before selecting Matthias as Judas Iscariot's successor (Acts 1:12–26). See also *Disciples of Jesus*; *Zealots*.

SISTERS OF JESUS. See *Brothers of Jesus*.

SKULL, THE. The site of Jesus's crucifixion (Mark 15:22; Luke 23:33). It is also known by its Latin name, *Calvary* (Luke 23:33 KJV) and its Aramaic name, *Golgotha* (Matthew 27:33; Mark 15:22; John 19:17).

In 1863 British general Charles Gordon identified a hill he believed could be "the Skull" described in Scripture—a rocky cliff face with deep crevices resembling eye sockets and a nose. The general popularized the site, now known as Gordon's Calvary, through his writings and lectures.

Not all Christians accept this hill as the site of the crucifixion. Catholics believe the more likely spot is inside an ancient church known as the Church of the Holy Sepulchre. Located within the walls of Jerusalem's Old City, the church is the successor to several other houses of worship that have been built here since AD 335. The site was first identified by Empress Helena, mother of the Roman emperor Constantine the Great, when she visited the Holy Land to identify all the sacred places associated with the life and ministry of Jesus. See also *Crucifixion*.

SLAUGHTER OF THE INNOCENTS. The attempt of Herod the Great to kill Jesus by ordering the elimination of all male infants in the region of Bethlehem (Matthew 2:16–18). This death order grew out of the Roman official's paranoia that a rival king had been born in Bethlehem. He hatched his evil plan when the Magi from the east stopped in Jerusalem and inquired where the "king of the Jews" had been born (Matthew 2:1–3). But the plot failed when Joseph and his family fled to Egypt after being warned of the danger by an angel (Matthew 2:13).

THE SERMON ON THE MOUNT

Herod's cruelty and disregard for human life has been well documented by secular historians. He murdered three members of his own family when he suspected they were a threat to his absolute power and authority. See also *Flight into Egypt*.

SON OF ABRAHAM. A name of Jesus that shows He was the fulfillment of the covenant God made with Abraham in Old Testament times. The name appears in the genealogy of Jesus in Matthew's gospel (1:1).

Many centuries before Jesus was born into the world, God called Abraham to begin the process of building a nation that would be devoted to the Lord. God promised to bless Abraham, but in turn his descendants, as the nation of Israel, were expected to serve as a blessing to the other nations of the world (Genesis 12:3).

The Jewish people eventually grew proud of their status as God's special people, and they conveniently forgot the second part of this covenant. But Jesus, as the son of Abraham, recovered the truth that God's plan of salvation included all people. He came as Savior for the entire world. See also *Genealogies of Jesus.*

SON OF DAVID. A name of Jesus that represents the fulfillment of a promise to King David that one of his descendants would always rule over God's people (2 Samuel 7:8-16). The name occurs in the very first verse of the New Testament, in Matthew's genealogy of Jesus, serving as a bridge between the Old and New Testaments (Matthew 1:1).

The Jewish people looked forward to the coming of the Messiah, expecting an earthly king and descendant of David who would return their nation to the days of glory it had enjoyed under David's rule. But Jesus refused to be this kind of king. He fulfilled God's promise to David in a spiritual sense by bringing in the kingdom of God. Jesus would serve as a ruler who delivered people from their bondage to sin. See also *Genealogies of Jesus.*

SON OF MAN. The name Jesus often used when referring to himself, as in "the Son of Man has no place to lay his head" (Luke 9:58) or "so the Son of Man must be lifted up" (John 3:14). In the Old Testament, God addressed the prophet Ezekiel by using this name (Ezekiel 2:1). The most basic meaning of this phrase is "human being" or "mortal."

Jesus may have called himself Son of Man to emphasize His role as a bold spokesman for God in the prophetic tradition of Ezekiel. Another possibility is that He used the name to call attention to His humanity and oneness with humankind. Jesus identified completely with the earth-bound people whom He had come into the world to save.

SONS OF THUNDER. A nickname that Jesus gave the fishermen brothers, James and John, soon after He enlisted them as His disciples (Mark 3:17). This is the meaning of the Greek word Jesus used, *Boanerges*.

The nickname probably referred to the bold, fiery spirit of the two brothers. They displayed this temperament when they encouraged Jesus to call down fire from heaven to destroy a group of Samaritans who refused to welcome Jesus to their village. Jesus rebuked them for their vengeful attitude (Luke 9:51-56).

SOWER AND SOILS PARABLE. See *Kingdom of God Parables.*

STAR OF BETHLEHEM. A mysterious star that appeared at the time Jesus was born. The wise men, or magi, from the east who presented gifts to the child Jesus interpreted this appearance as a sign of a royal birth among the Jewish people (Matthew 2:2-10).

These wise men were probably impressed by this star because they practiced the ancient art of astrology. They believed the heavenly bodies determined—or at least held important clues—about the future and a person's destiny.

This mysterious star has been the object of much specula-tion. Some interpreters explain it scientifically—as a comet or the result of two or more planets moving close together to create an unusually bright light in the sky.

But this theory fails to explain the star's strange behavior. It first appeared to the wise men in their homeland, but no men-tion is made of it again until they were "overjoyed" by seeing it a second time in Jerusalem (verse 10). The star "went ahead of them" to Bethlehem and stopped over the place "where the child [Jesus] was" (verse 9).

An odd star, indeed. The only logical explanation is that it was a miracle from a miracle-working God, announcing the miracu-lous birth in Bethlehem. See also *Magi.*

STAR OUT OF JACOB. A name of Jesus that was spoken by Balaam, a pagan magician, several centuries before Jesus was born (Numbers 24:17). Balaam foretold that this "star," or prince, would subdue all the enemies of the people of Israel. Many Bible students interpret this title as a reference to the Messiah, who would rule over God's people with divine authority and power.

Balaam was hired by the pagan king of Moab to curse the Israelites as they passed through his territory during the exodus from Egypt. But under the influence of God, Balaam blessed the Israelites instead, and issued this prophecy of the Messiah. See also *Messianic Prophecies.*

STONE PAVEMENT. A broad paved area near the temple in Jerusalem where Pilate pronounced the death penalty against Jesus (John 19:13-16). The Aramaic word for this place is *Gabbatha,* meaning "an elevated place."

The reputed site of this sentencing is included today in the Via Dolorosa, the "way of sorrows" that Jesus followed on His way to the cross. Beneath the Sisters of Zion convent, visitors are shown ancient flagstones that are said to be a part of the pavement where Jesus was condemned to death. See also *Via Dolorosa.*

STONES INTO BREAD. See *Temptations of Jesus.*

STONES WILL CRY OUT. See *Triumphal Entry into Jerusalem.*

STUMBLING BLOCK. A phrase used by the apostle Paul to describe the reluctance of many Jews to place their faith in Jesus because of His crucifixion (1 Corinthians 1:23). They found it hard to believe that the long-expected Messiah would be executed like a common criminal. But to Paul, Jesus's atoning death expressed the love of God for a sinful world.

SUFFERING SERVANT. See *Isaiah*.

SUSANNA. A woman who provided material support for Jesus and His disciples during His ministry in Galilee (Luke 8:3). This is the only mention of Susanna in the Bible.

SWADDLING CLOTHES. Strips of cloth wrapped around the body of the newborn Jesus—a common custom in New Testament times. See also *Bethlehem*.

SYCAMORE TREE. See *Zacchaeus*.

SYCHAR. A village near the well where Jesus talked with a Samaritan woman and offered her living water (John 4:5-40). This name is similar to that of modern-day Askar, an Arab village not far from the purported well where Jesus encountered the woman. See also *Jacob's Well*.

SYNAGOGUE. A place where the Jewish people gathered for worship and study of the Old Testament Scriptures. In the synagogue at Nazareth, Jesus's hometown, He read a passage from the writings of Isaiah and identified himself as the Suffering Servant described by the prophet (Luke 4:16-21). See also *Isaiah*.

SYNOPTIC GOSPELS. A phrase designating the first three gospels—Matthew, Mark, and Luke—because of their similarity.

The word *synoptic* comes from a Greek word that means "to see together." These gospels contain accounts of many of the same events from the life of Jesus and often parallel one another with just minor differences in wording and factual detail.

Scholars theorize that the gospel of Mark was written first, and that Matthew and Luke followed Mark's pattern, even including some material from Mark almost verbatim. But Matthew and Luke also contain information not found in Mark, or any other gospel. For example, only Luke tells us about the birth of Jesus in Bethlehem (Luke 2:1-7). And Matthew alone reports Jesus's parable of the unforgiving servant (Matthew 18:23-35).

The gospel of John is not considered synoptic, because it is so different from the first three gospels in the way it treats the life and ministry of Jesus. For example, John does not contain a single major parable of Jesus. Instead of focusing on the events in Jesus's life, the fourth gospel goes behind the scenes to give us the deeper meaning of many of these happenings. See also *John, Gospel of.*

TABERNACLES. See *Feast of Tabernacles.*

TABOR. See *Mount Tabor.*

TAKE UP ONE'S CROSS. A metaphor that Jesus used to show the level of commitment required of those who follow Him. To "take up the cross" means to deny the self and to be willing to endure suffering, criticism, and rejection in order to serve Jesus (Matthew 16:24-25).

The gospels of Matthew and Luke record this saying of Jesus, and Luke adds the word *daily* (Luke 9:23). Following Jesus does not consist of isolated moments of sacrifice, but an entire life devoted to the commands of God and the needs of those He has commissioned us to serve.

On one occasion, Jesus was approached by a man who wanted to become a follower but had not considered the cost of doing so. "Foxes have dens, and birds of the sky have nests," Jesus replied, "but the Son of Man has no place to lay His head" (Luke 9:58 HCSB). Jesus wanted the man to realize that following Him required great sacrifice—even to the point of giving up personal comfort and security.

TALENTS PARABLE. Jesus told about a landowner who gave three servants different sums of money—talents in the King James Version, bags of gold in the New International Version—to manage in his absence. The first servant received ten talents, the second got two, and the third was entrusted with one. The first two servants managed wisely and doubled the value of their money. But the third servant played it safe and hid his one talent in the ground. This action obviously produced no return (Matthew 25:14-30).

When the landowner returned, he commended the two servants who had invested wisely. But he had harsh words for the unproductive servant. The landowner took away the third servant's one talent, giving it to the servant who had doubled his five talents into ten. "Whoever has will be given more," Jesus declared, "and they will have an abundance" (verse 29).

The message of this parable is that God expects Christians to be wise stewards of their talents—both in the sense of the material goods and the personal abilities He has given them. When people cultivate these gifts and use them in God's service, they will be multiplied and result in a great reward. But the opposite is also true: God-given talents not employed for Him will waste away like an unused muscle, eventually becoming useless and non-productive. See also *Minas Parable*.

TAX COLLECTOR. A Jewish citizen who collected tax revenue from His fellow Jews for the Roman government (Mark 2:16; *publican*: KJV). The Jewish people hated these agents, considering them pawns of the enemy who preyed on the land and its people.

Jesus was criticized by the Pharisees for associating with tax collectors and other outcasts of society. He even called a tax collector named Matthew to become one of His disciples (Matthew 9:9-13). He also accepted Zacchaeus, a chief tax collector, who agreed to repay the people he had cheated through his tax collection practices (Luke 19:1-10). See also *Matthew*; *Zacchaeus*.

TEACHER OF THE LAW. See *Expert in the Law.*

TEACHING METHOD OF JESUS. See *Parables of Jesus.*

TEMPLE. The central place of worship in Jerusalem that symbolized God's presence for the Jewish people. In Jesus's time, this building was being expanded and remodeled into a more ornate structure. Herod the Great, Roman ruler over Palestine, had begun the project years before to curry favor with his Jewish subjects.

THE TWELVE DISCIPLES

Disciples of Jesus

Andrew

James, Brother of John

James, Son of Alphaeus

John the Apostle

Judas Iscariot

Matthew

Matthias

Nathanael

Peter

Philip, Disciple of Jesus

Simon the Zealot

Thaddaeus

Thomas

This building impressed the disciples because of its beautiful stonework (Luke 21:5-6). But Jesus declared it was all for nothing, saying that this beautiful building would be destroyed—a prediction fulfilled about forty years later when the Roman army sacked Jerusalem.

Jesus showed He was superior to the temple when He cleansed it of merchants and moneychangers (Mark 11:15-17). He also stated that if the temple of His body was destroyed, He would raise it up in three days—a reference to His resurrection (John 2:19-22).

This statement was misinterpreted and used against Jesus in His trial before the Jewish Sanhedrin. Two witnesses testified that He was referring to the physical temple and was thus guilty of blasphemous words against God and His sacred place (Mark 15:29). See also *Cleanses the Temple*.

TEMPTATIONS OF JESUS. Satan's attempt, at the beginning of Jesus's public ministry, to convince Him to accomplish His mission in a way other than God intended. Three distinct temptations are recorded by the gospel writers (Matthew 4:1-11; Luke 4:1-13).

The first temptation was for Jesus to use divine power to meet His own physical needs—to turn stones into bread to satisfy His hunger. Another dimension of this temptation was for Jesus to become a "bread Messiah," to entice people to follow Him by providing food for their bodies.

Temptation number two was for Jesus to jump from the highest point of the temple in Jerusalem into the deep canyon below, allowing the angels to protect Him from injury. The crowds would be sure to follow Him, Satan implied, if He dazzled them with a spectacular stunt like this.

The third temptation was actually a promise. If the Lord would worship Satan, the devil said he would give Jesus "all the kingdoms of the world" (Luke 4:5-7). Satan was offering Jesus an easy way out, a chance to avoid the bitter path to the cross, using His divine power to become rich and enjoy a life of leisure.

Jesus resisted all these temptations by relying on His heavenly Father and the principles He quoted from Scripture. This victory over Satan's enticements showed that Jesus was ready to begin His mission as Savior of the world.

TEN MEN WITH LEPROSY HEALED. See *Leprosy.*

TEN VIRGINS PARABLE. See *Second Coming.*

THADDAEUS. A disciple of Jesus who is listed among the Twelve (Matthew 10:2-4; Mark 3:14-19) but mentioned only one additional time in the Gospels. He is apparently the same disciple identified as Judas, son of James, in the gospel of Luke (6:13-16) and the book of Acts (1:13-14).

In John's gospel, this disciple questioned Jesus about how He would show himself to His disciples and not to the world. John, who used the name Judas, was careful to identify this as a different disciple than Judas Iscariot, who betrayed Jesus (John 14:22).

To add to the confusion about the exact identity of this disciple, the King James Version calls him "Lebbaeus, whose surname was Thaddaeus" (Matthew 10:3). See also *Disciples of Jesus.*

THEOPHILUS. The person to whom Luke addressed his two-part work—the gospel of Luke (1:1-4) and the book of Acts (1:1). Since Luke addressed him as "most excellent Theophilus" (Luke 1:3), he may have been a high official of the Roman government. His name means "lover of God," but nothing else is known of the man.

Some have speculated that Theophilus was an unbelieving friend to whom Luke addressed his writings, in hopes of convincing the man to become a Christian. But there is no evidence to support this theory. See also *Luke, Gospel of.*

THIEF ON THE CROSS. In the King James Version of the Bible, the Synoptic Gospels report that Jesus was crucified between two thieves, or malefactors (Matthew 27:38-44; Mark 15:27-28; Luke 23:32-43). The New International Version uses the terms *rebels* or *criminals.* Luke's gospel is the only account to note that one of the criminals came to believe in Jesus while they both hung on crosses.

This man admitted that he and the other lawbreaker were receiving the punishment they deserved. But he recognized that Jesus was suffering a great injustice. In that desperate hour, the man believed in Jesus. He must have realized that the man on the center cross was the Messiah who had promised to establish the kingdom of God, and he asked Jesus to remember him when He ushered in this kingdom.

Jesus did more than this thief requested, assuring him that they would be together in paradise that very day.

By executing Jesus between two common criminals, the Roman authorities were probably trying to humiliate Him, to make Him an object lesson to potential lawbreakers. But their deliberate action brought about the fulfillment of an ancient prophecy. Several centuries before Jesus was born, the prophet Isaiah had predicted that the Messiah would be "numbered with the transgressors" (Isaiah 53:12). See also *Messianic Prophecies.*

THIRTY PIECES OF SILVER. See *Judas Iscariot.*

THOMAS. The disciple who demanded to see and touch the piercings in Jesus's hands and feet before he would believe in the resurrection (John 20:24-29). Because of this insistence on material proof, he is often referred to as "doubting Thomas." When Jesus appeared and invited Thomas to put his fingers into

Jesus's wounds, the disciple did recognize Him as "my Lord and my God" (verse 28).

In a previous incident recorded in John's gospel, Thomas comes across more positively. Jesus was determined to go to Bethany to raise His friend Lazarus from the dead. The disciples were hesitant to accompany Jesus because the Jewish religious leaders in nearby Jerusalem were plotting to put Him to death. But Thomas encouraged his fellow disciples with brave words: "Let us also go," he declared, "that we may die with him" (John 11:16).

Thomas is also referred to as *Didymus,* a Greek word that means "Twin" (John 11:16). See also *Disciples of Jesus.*

T

TIBERIAS. See *Sea of Galilee.*

TIBERIUS CAESAR. Roman emperor when John the Baptist launched his public ministry (Luke 3:1). Tiberius succeeded Caesar Augustus, who was emperor of Rome when Jesus was born (Luke 2:1). The city of Tiberias (John 6:23) on the shore of the Sea of Galilee was named for Tiberius. See also *Roman Empire.*

TRANSFIGURATION OF JESUS. The dramatic change in Jesus's appearance that occurred on a mountain before three of His disciples—Peter, James, and John. This occurred about a week after Peter's great confession of Jesus as the Messiah (Luke 9:28-36).

These disciples apparently had no warning that this spectacular event was about to happen. As Jesus was praying, "the appearance of his face changed, and his clothes became as bright as a flash of lightning" (verse 29).

This strange transformation was a preview of what Jesus had told His disciples several times—that He would be glorified by God the Father, be received into heaven, and then return to earth one day in all His glory (Matthew 25:31). Perhaps He was giving these disciples a glimpse of His glorified body to encourage and strengthen them for the hard-to-believe events that were drawing near—His crucifixion, death, and resurrection.

To make this scene even more unusual, two of the greatest personalities of the Old Testament—Moses and Elijah—appeared and talked with Jesus. Then, after they disappeared, a cloud surrounded Jesus and the three disciples. Out of the cloud came the voice of God the Father: "This is my Son, whom I have chosen; listen to him" (Luke 9:35).

These three disciples must have obeyed this voice and paid attention to the words and teachings of Jesus. After His ascension, they became faithful witnesses in the early church in Jerusalem. See also *Mount Tabor.*

TREASURES IN HEAVEN. A phrase from Jesus's Sermon on the Mount that focuses on the source of true security. The Lord emphasized that treasures on earth—earthly possessions that most people labor a lifetime to accumulate—can be taken away at any time. Only the treasures we build up in heaven, through service to Jesus and His kingdom, will last forever (Matthew 6:20).

Jesus went on to declare, "Where your treasure is, there your heart will be also" (Matthew 6:21). In other words, we will concentrate our time and attention on the things we value most.

Citizens of God's kingdom realize that this world and its values are not the most important things in life. What really matters are such everyday actions as spreading kindness and joy, extending a helping hand to others, building strong relationships with family and friends, introducing others to Jesus, and serving the Lord with gladness. See also *Possessions.*

TRIALS OF JESUS. A series of four court appearances to which Jesus was subjected before He was sentenced to die by Pontius Pilate. In the first two trials, Jesus stood before the

Jewish religious leaders, while the other two took place before Roman authorities. Here's a brief summary of these trials, based on a careful reading of all four gospels:

1. Preliminary hearing before Annas, father-in-law of the reigning high priest Caiaphas, and several members of the Sanhedrin. Annas may have made the decision to have Jesus stand trial before the full Jewish court (John 18:12-24).

2. Official hearing before the entire Sanhedrin, with the high priest Caiaphas presiding. Their verdict was that Jesus was guilty of blasphemy against God and deserved to die. But the Sanhedrin did not have the authority to put a person to death, and they realized that a religious offense was not sufficient grounds for capital punishment. So they forwarded Jesus to Pilate with the charge that He was guilty of rebellion against the Roman government, refusing to pay taxes to Rome, and claiming to be a king (Matthew 26:57-68; 27:1-2; Luke 22:66-23:2).

3. First appearance before Pilate, Roman governor of Judea. Believing Jesus to be innocent of the charges against Him, Pilate tried to pass off responsibility by sending Him off to Herod Antipas. This Herod, Roman governor of Galilee, happened to be in Jerusalem that day for the Passover celebration. Antipas questioned Jesus but refused to rule in His case and sent Him back to Pilate (Luke 23:3-12).

4. Second appearance before Pilate. Bowing to pressure from the Jewish religious leaders, Pilate finally pronounced the death sentence against Jesus and delivered Him to a detachment of soldiers to be crucified (Matthew 27:15-26). See also *Pilate*; *Sanhedrin*.

TRIUMPHAL ENTRY INTO JERUSALEM. Jesus's entry into Jerusalem to the jubilation of the crowds, who welcomed Him as the long-awaited Messiah. They greeted Him with the shout, "Hosanna to the son of David!" (Matthew 21:9). *Hosanna* means "God save us."

Some Pharisees in the crowd urged Jesus to tell the people to quiet down. But Jesus responded, "If these should hold their peace, the stones would immediately cry out" (Luke 19:40 KJV). It was inevitable that Jesus be recognized and honored as God's agent of redemption. If people refused to do so, the lifeless stones would.

This enthusiastic greeting shows the people thought of Jesus as an earthly king who would defeat the enemies of the Jews and restore their nation to the glory days of the past. But Jesus entered the city on a donkey, symbolizing His humility—that He was a spiritual deliverer, not the military conqueror they wanted Him to be.

Jesus entered Jerusalem on a Sunday while people were celebrating the Jewish Passover. During this major national holiday, expectations of the coming of the Messiah always ran high. Just five days later, Jesus was crucified, and the fickle crowd turned against Him. Their enthusiastic welcome turned into anger and resentment when He refused to live up to their expectations.

The Sunday that Jesus rode into Jerusalem is commemorated as Palm Sunday during the Easter season. The name comes from the palm branches that people placed in Jesus's path as He entered the city (Matthew 21:8; John 12:13).

According to Matthew's gospel, Jesus's entry on a donkey was the fulfillment of a prophecy from the Old Testament prophet Zechariah: "See, your king comes to you . . . lowly and riding on a donkey" (Zechariah 9:9; see Matthew 21:5). See also *Holy Week*.

TRUE VINE. A name of Jesus that emphasizes the need for all believers to draw their inspiration and strength from Him. Jesus used this name for himself on the night before He was arrested, anticipating that the disciples would need His strength during the upcoming crisis (John 15:1–8).

By speaking of himself as the True Vine, Jesus claimed to be superior to the nation of Israel, which was often referred to as a vine (Isaiah 5:7). God's chosen people of the Old Testament were supposed to bear witness of Him to the rest of the world. But they became proud of their heritage, separated themselves from the Gentiles, and failed to fulfill this divine mission. So Jesus was the True Vine who bore the fruit that God desired by bringing salvation to a dark world.

The vine imagery that Jesus used was probably drawn from the grapevine, one of the most important plants in Israel. This plant had a main stem rooted in the ground, and the stem gave life to smaller branches from which grapes were harvested.

Believers need to stay attached to Jesus—the main stem known as the True Vine. He will sustain and nourish His people so they can bear fruit for Him as His witnesses in the world. See also *Remain in Me*.

TURNS WATER INTO WINE. This miracle—Jesus's first, according to the gospel of John—occurred at a wedding to which He and His disciples had been invited. Mary, the mother of Jesus, was also present. His family probably knew the hosts at this celebration since Cana, the village where it occurred, was just a few miles from their hometown of Nazareth (John 2:1–11).

Soon after Jesus arrived, Mary told Him that the host family had run out of wine. Jesus asked her, "Why do you involve me?" Then He said, "My hour has not yet come" (verse 4). He probably thought this was not the time or place to demonstrate His power as the divine Son of God. But then He changed His mind and transformed common water into wine to protect the host family from embarrassment.

The most interesting detail in this miracle is that Jesus produced wine from the water in six stone pots which were "used by the Jews for ceremonial washing" (verse 6). The people thought elaborate washing of the hands kept them ceremonially clean and made them acceptable to God. Jesus's miracle dramatized the inadequacy of this ritual, declaring that faith in Him was the only way to God's favor.

TWELVE, THE. See *Disciples of Jesus.*

TWO BLIND MEN HEALED. Once, as Jesus walked along, two blind men groped their way after Him. They had probably heard how He had healed other people of their disabilities. Even though they cried out loudly for mercy, Jesus kept walking until He entered a house. When the two men followed Him in, He took this as evidence of their faith, touching their eyes and restoring their sight (Matthew 9:27–31).

Jesus warned the men not to tell anyone what had happened. He probably wanted to avoid idle speculation about His miracles among the crowds, who were looking for a powerful king to restore the fortunes of their nation. His mission was to be a spiritual deliverer.

TWO SONS AND A VINEYARD PARABLE. This short parable is about a father and his two sons. The father asked both to work in his vineyard. One son refused to do so but then changed his mind and went. The second son agreed to go but didn't follow through (Matthew 21:28–32).

Jesus asked his audience, which included several Jewish religious leaders, which son had done what the father wanted. They had to agree it was the first. Jesus then applied the parable to these officials of the Jewish establishment: they were represented by the second son. Just like him, these people promised to do God's will. But they refused to believe John the Baptist or the Messiah whose arrival John announced.

The son who did go to work in the vineyard represented those people the religious leaders considered sinners and unworthy of God's love. These outcasts believed John the Baptist and the

Messiah and repented of their sins. They were the people who had done God's will and followed His commands.

UNCLEAN SPIRITS. See *Demons and Demon Possession*.

UNFORGIVING SERVANT PARABLE. This parable grew out of a question that Peter asked Jesus about forgiveness. Peter wanted to know how many times a citizen of God's kingdom should forgive a person who had sinned against him. Jesus replied that forgiveness has no limits, and He related this parable to show its importance in the life of a believer (Matthew 18:21–35).

Jesus told about a king who showed mercy toward one of his servants who owed him a huge sum of money. It was impossible for this loan ever to be repaid, so the king just wrote off the debt. But the servant failed to show the same spirit of mercy to a fellow servant who owed him some money. It was a small sum compared to the huge debt the king had dismissed.

When the king heard about this, he summoned the servant into his presence, gave him a tongue lashing, and reinstated the debt. Then the king threw the man into prison, swearing that he would not be released until he had paid every penny he owed.

This parable shows that forgiveness is a two-way street. Since God has forgiven us, He expects us to show forgiveness toward others. There is no place in the kingdom of God for a harsh, unforgiving spirit.

UNIVERSAL REIGN OF JESUS. A truth expressed by the apostle John in the book of Revelation, that Jesus will rule over all creation at the end of the age. John expressed it like this: "The kingdom of the world has become the kingdom of our Lord and of his Messiah, and he will reign for ever and ever" (Revelation 11:15).

T
U

Later in the book, John saw in a vision that Jesus will return to earth in glory as King of Kings and Lord of Lords. On His head will be many crowns, symbolizing His dominion over all the nations of the earth (Revelation 19:11–16). See also *Second Coming.*

UNJUST JUDGE PARABLE. See *Persistent Widow Parable.*

UNJUST STEWARD. See *Shrewd Manager Parable.*

UNLEAVENED BREAD. See *Feast of Passover.*

UNPARDONABLE SIN. See *Blasphemy against the Holy Spirit.*

UPPER ROOM. A large room in a building in Jerusalem where Jesus ate the Last Supper with His disciples, just before His arrest. It was probably a guest room in a private home owned by one of His followers. Jesus knew about this room and sent two of His disciples to find its owner and ask permission to use it (Mark 14:13–15).

Two sites in Jerusalem are reputed to be the place where this event occurred. The first is a large rectangular hall known as the *Cenaculum,* a name derived from a Latin word meaning "dinner." The second place is marked by a small church known as the Church of Saint Mark. Both shrines are successors to several other buildings that have been erected across the centuries to mark this sacred spot. See also *Lord's Supper.*

VIA DOLOROSA. The Latin name, meaning "Way of Sorrows," for the route Jesus took through Jerusalem on the way to His crucifixion. The name does not appear in the Bible.

Twelve "stations of the cross," indicating places where significant events are said to have occurred, are marked along this path through Old Jerusalem's narrow streets. But it is impossible to determine the exact course that Jesus followed, since Jerusalem has been destroyed and rebuilt several times since the New Testament era.

VINE. See *True Vine.*

VINEYARD. A field where grapes were grown. These plots were common throughout Palestine, whose soil and climate were ideal for grape production. Vineyards have a prominent role in three of Jesus's parables. See *Two Sons and a Vineyard Parable*; *Wicked Tenants in a Vineyard Parable*; *Workers in a Vineyard Parable*.

VIRGIN BIRTH. The doctrine that Jesus was born to a woman, Mary, who had never had sex with a man. Actually, the terms "virginal conception" or "miraculous conception" are more descriptive of what took place. Jesus was conceived in Mary's womb by the Holy Spirit, but He was born through the normal biological process that brings children into the world (Luke 1:26-38).

This process was just as puzzling for Mary as it is for us today. The angel Gabriel explained to her that in some mysterious way God would "overshadow" her by His Spirit to bring about a miraculous conception (verse 35).

This goes against human reason and natural law, but God chose to make an exception to the human reproductive process to bring about the birth of the Savior of the world.

The doctrine of the virgin birth emphasizes the dual existence of Jesus. His divine nature as God's Son was joined with His human nature in an earthly mother's womb. From the very beginning, He was the God-man—both fully human and fully divine. See also *Annunciation of Jesus's Birth*; *Mary, Mother of Jesus*.

VARIOUS TEACHINGS OF JESUS

WALKS ON THE WATER. Soon after Jesus's miraculous feeding of the five thousand, His disciples got into a small fishing boat and headed to the other side of the Sea of Galilee. Jesus stayed behind on a mountainside to meditate and pray (Matthew 14:22–33).

A sudden storm struck the lake and threatened to swamp the boat. Jesus must have realized the disciples were in danger, so He went out to meet them. When the disciples saw His ghostly form walking on the violent waves in the midst of the storm, they were terrified.

Jesus identified himself, saying, "Take courage! . . . Don't be afraid" (verse 27). Peter wanted to walk out to meet Him, and as long as he kept his eyes on Jesus, he stayed on top of the water. But when Peter looked away in fear, because of the howling wind, he began to sink. Jesus grabbed Peter's hand and pulled him back to the surface, reproving Peter's weak faith.

As soon as Jesus and Peter climbed into the boat, the storm died down and the churning waters grew calm. The disciples were impressed by this dramatic demonstration of Jesus's power, bowing before Him in worship to declare, "Truly you are the Son of God" (verse 33). In this moment, recognizing Jesus's unlimited power, they took a big step forward in understanding who He was. See also *Calms a Storm.*

WARS AND RUMORS OF WARS. See *Olivet Discourse.*

WASHES THE DISCIPLES' FEET. Washing a guest's feet was a gesture of hospitality in New Testament times. This task was usually performed by a household servant. But Jesus took the role for himself when He washed the disciples' feet on the night they ate the Passover meal together (John 13:1–17).

Luke's gospel establishes the setting for this event. When Jesus gathered with His disciples for the meal, "a dispute also arose among them as to which of them was considered to be greatest" (Luke 22:24). Even on the eve of Jesus's death, the twelve were squabbling over matters of earthly pride and prominence.

Through this lowly act, Jesus demonstrated what He had tried to drill into the disciples for more than three years—that true greatness consists of humble service to others. And He went on to tell them that His example of service toward them should become the pattern of their lives.

This action of Jesus has an important message for all believers. For anyone tempted to think that some forms of service are beneath them, the antidote is to think of Jesus with a towel around His waist, kneeling at the feet of His disciples during the final hours of His life on earth. See also *Lord's Supper.*

WATER INTO WINE. See *Turns Water into Wine.*

W

WAY OF SORROWS. See *Via Dolorosa*.

WEDDING BANQUET PARABLE. In this parable, a king invited people to attend a feast to celebrate the wedding of his son. Everyone agreed to come. But when the king sent word that the celebration was about to begin, they refused to attend (Matthew 22:1-10).

In New Testament times, an invitation was sent several weeks before an event to determine how many guests to prepare for. Then a second invitation went out on the day of the celebration to those who had agreed to attend.

Through this parable, Jesus emphasized that His offer of salvation went first to His own people, the Jews. But they refused to accept it. Just as the king in the story invited people off the street to replace those who would not attend, Jesus now issued His invitation—salvation—to the Gentiles. See also *Great Banquet Parable*.

W

WHEAT AND WEEDS. See *Kingdom of God Parables*.

WHO IS MY NEIGHBOR? See *Good Samaritan Parable*.

WICKED ONE. See *Satan*.

WICKED TENANTS IN A VINEYARD PARABLE. Jesus told a parable about a landowner who planted a vineyard and leased it to tenants. Their responsibility was to make it productive and return a portion of the crop to the vineyard owner (Luke 20:9-19).

After the harvest was gathered, the owner sent three servants at different times to claim his share of the crop. But the tenants beat up these servants and refused to pay what they owed. Finally, the landowner sent his own son to confront the deadbeat tenants and settle the debt. But the tenants murdered the son, thinking the vineyard would fall into their hands.

Jesus applied the message of the parable by quoting from the psalms: "The stone the builders rejected has become the cornerstone" (Luke 20:17; see Psalm 118:22). This was a reference to His own impending death at the hands of the Jewish religious leaders, who were represented by the wicked tenants. Jesus meant that the rejected Messiah would become the universal Savior—the cornerstone—who would deliver humankind from its bondage to sin.

The religious leaders in Jesus's audience realized that this parable was directed at them. They became even more determined to have Him arrested, but because of Jesus's popularity with the common people, their plans were foiled for the time being.

WIDOW'S MITE. See *Widow's Sacrificial Offering.*

W

WIDOW'S SACRIFICIAL OFFERING. Jesus watched as people dropped their voluntary offerings into a collection box in the temple. Many wealthy people put in large amounts. But Jesus commended only a poor widow who dropped in two small coins (*mites:* KJV). These were the smallest of the thin brass coins of that time; two would be valued at just a few cents (Mark 12:41–44).

The woman's meager offering was actually greater than all the others being given, Jesus told His disciples, because she gave out of all proportion to her resources. She put in "all she had to live on" (verse 44).

One irony we often overlook in this event is that this woman had *two* coins—she could have kept one for herself, but she gave both. The point of this account is that true Christian giving is sacrificial in nature. God measures our gifts not by their size but by our level of devotion to Him. Total commitment to the Lord always results in generous giving.

WIDOW'S SON RAISED FROM THE DEAD. Jesus and His disciples were visiting the village of Nain, about twenty-five miles south of Capernaum. As they entered the town, they met a group of mourners carrying the body of a young man for burial outside the village (Luke 7:11–17).

This young man was the only son of a woman who had already lost her husband. Jesus realized immediately the gravity of her loss, the consequences to a woman left with no means of support. In a burst of compassion, He urged her not to cry. Then He brought the young man back to life and presented him to his mother.

News about this miracle spread throughout the region. The common people recognized that God had sent a great prophet to minister among His people.

This name is similar to that of the modern village of Nein, an Arab town reputed to mark the biblical site. Here Jesus's miracle is memorialized by the Church of the Resurrection of the Widow's Son, a beautiful little chapel built during the 1800s by the Catholic Franciscan order.

WILD MAN AMONG THE TOMBS HEALED. See *Demons and Demon Possession*, No. 1.

WINESKIN. A vessel fashioned from animal skins and used to hold liquids such as wine and water. With age, wineskins grew brittle and could not hold new wine, since it expanded during the fermentation process. So Jesus declared, "No one pours new wine into old wineskins. Otherwise, the new wine will burst the skins" (Luke 5:37; *bottles:* KJV).

Jesus was saying that the old era of the law was not compatible with the new age of grace that He brought into the world. Just as old wineskins would not hold new wine, so Jesus's teachings required a radical break from the traditions of the past.

WISE MEN. See *Magi.*

WITHERED HAND. See *Man with Deformed Hand Healed.*

WITNESS. See *Great Commission*; *High Priestly Prayer of Jesus*; *Mediator.*

WOES AGAINST THE PHARISEES. Jesus pronounced a series of seven woes against the Pharisees, His perpetual enemies, in Matthew 23. For this reason, this passage is often referred to as the "woe chapter" of the New Testament.

In this long monologue, Jesus condemned the Pharisees for their hypocrisy, self-righteousness, pride, and greed. He also criticized the way they made a show of their fastidious observance of the law, hindered people from entering the kingdom of God, and majored on legalistic religious rituals while ignoring more important matters such as justice and mercy. See also *Pharisees.*

W

WOLVES IN SHEEP'S CLOTHING. A phrase for false prophets, from Jesus's Sermon on the Mount. See *Sermon on the Mount,* No. 8.

WOMAN ACCUSED OF ADULTERY. See *Adultery.*

WOMAN AT THE WELL. The unnamed woman to whom Jesus offered living water at Jacob's well in Samaria. Their conversation began when Jesus asked her to draw Him a drink, but it quickly moved into a deep discussion of spiritual matters (John 4:1-42).

The woman was surprised that Jesus would talk with her, since Jews did not normally associate with Samaritans. She was also amazed that He knew all about her turbulent past and her marriage to five different husbands. Jesus assured the woman that she could turn her life around by drinking the spiritual water that He offered to sinful people.

We are never told specifically that this woman accepted the spiritual redemption that Jesus offered. But her actions after she left the well suggest that she did. The woman told everyone in her village about the man "who told me everything I ever did" (verse 29). A person radically changed by Jesus is eager to share this news with others. See also *Jacob's Well*; *Samaria*.

WOMAN WITH CROOKED BACK HEALED. See *Demons and Demon Possession*, No. 7.

WOMAN WITH HEMORRHAGE HEALED. Jesus was on His way to heal the daughter of Jairus, a synagogue leader, when He was spotted among the crowd by a woman with a desperate need of her own. She had been losing blood for twelve years (Mark 5:25-34).

This debilitating condition was made even worse by its social consequences. According to the Old Testament law, the woman was considered ceremonially unclean. The social norms of her time kept her from finding God's favor (Leviticus 15:25-30).

This woman believed that Jesus could heal her, but she was reluctant to confront Him face-to-face. So she slipped through the crowd and touched His cloak. Immediately, the woman was healed.

At her touch, Jesus felt power flow from His body. This tells us that healing people cost Him something—restoring a person to wholeness took something out of Jesus's reservoir of divine power. But He was willing to pay this price to help people who were in extreme need.

Jesus turned to the crowd and asked, "Who touched my clothes?" (verse 30). Trembling with fear, the woman came forward, fell at His feet, and confessed that she was the one. But Jesus had not called out the woman to embarrass her; He wanted the crowd to understand that she was now ceremonially clean— she could participate freely in community activities and worship of the Lord. Jesus calmed the woman's fears, announcing that her faith had delivered her from her long years of embarrassment and social isolation.

WOMAN WITH ISSUE OF BLOOD. See *Woman with Hemorrhage Healed.*

WOMEN AT THE CROSS AND TOMB. In New Testament times, women were looked upon as second-class citizens who had few rights, little influence, and even less credibility. But Jesus rejected this stereotype by respecting women, healing them of their disabilities, and welcoming them as His followers.

Several women responded to Jesus's open-minded attitude by following Him all the way to the cross and the empty tomb. They showed more bravery than most of the twelve male disciples, who struggled with fear and unbelief.

These loyal women are mentioned throughout the Gospels. They include several women named Mary: Mary, Jesus's own mother (John 19:25); Mary Magdalene, who is mentioned at the cross and tomb in all four gospels (Matthew 27:61; 28:1; Mark 15:40; 16:1; Luke 24:9-10; John 19:25; 20:1); Mary, mother of James and John (Matthew 27:55-56; 28:1); Mary, mother of James the younger (a disciple of Jesus) and of Joseph (Mark 15:40-41);

W

Mary, wife of Clopas (John 19:25); Salome (Mark 15:40–41; 16:1); and Joanna (Luke 24:10).

Little else is known about several of these women, but see *Joanna; Mary Magdalene; Mary, Mother of Jesus; Salome*.

WONDERFUL COUNSELOR. A messianic title of Jesus that points to His perfect wisdom and sound guidance. The name appears in a familiar passage from the prophet Isaiah that is often read at Christmas time (9:6).

A counselor is one who offers wise instruction to others. Jesus is the source of divine wisdom. His guidance is available to all believers through the leading of the Holy Spirit, through the counsel of fellow Christians, and through the principles found in the Bible, the written Word of God.

WORDS WILL NEVER PASS AWAY. A phrase that Jesus used to contrast the fleeting nature of earthly things with the eternal values of the kingdom of God (Mark 13:31). Even the earth as we know it would eventually come to an end, but the truths He taught about His kingdom would last forever.

Jesus also referred to the certainty of His prediction about the end of time. The words He spoke about the end of the age would most certainly come to pass, whenever God the Father chose.

In His Sermon on the Mount, Jesus also referred to the permanence of His teachings when He declared, "One jot or one tittle shall in no wise pass from the law, till all be fulfilled" (Matthew 5:18 KJV). The word *jot* refers to the smallest letter of the Greek alphabet. A *tittle* was a small mark used to highlight the difference between similarly shaped letters of the Hebrew alphabet.

WORKERS IN A VINEYARD PARABLE. This parable is a continuation of Jesus's discussion with His disciples about the reward they could expect for following Him. Jesus told them about a vineyard owner who hired several separate groups of laborers at different times throughout the day to work in his vineyard. At the end of the day, he paid all of them the same wage, no matter how many hours they had worked (Matthew 20:1–16).

The laborers who had worked all day considered this unfair. But the vineyard owner replied that he had paid them exactly what he had promised. "I want to give the one who was hired last the same as I gave you," he explained. "Are you envious because I am generous?" (verses 14–15).

The disciples must have been thinking they had given up a lot to follow Jesus. But through this parable He cautioned them not to be envious of believers in the years ahead who would enter God's kingdom without making the sacrifice the twelve had made. These future followers would make their own unique contribution to the work of the Lord, and God would honor them in His own gracious fashion.

This parable also teaches that Christians should devote their lives to God not because they expect a reward but instead for the pure joy of serving Him.

WORRY. See *Kingdom of God.*

W

YEAST IN DOUGH. See *Kingdom of God Parables.*

Y

YOKE IS EASY. A statement of Jesus which declared that following Him is easy in comparison to the burdensome rules and petty regulations of the Pharisees (Matthew 11:30). A yoke around the neck of an ox enabled it to pull a plow. In Jesus's time, the yoke was a metaphor for submission to a rabbinical teacher. To be yoked with Jesus is to be fitted for a life of service that is easy to bear because He walks with us and gives us strength for the journey.

ZACCHAEUS. A tax collector from Jericho who climbed a tree to see Jesus as He passed through the city on His last trip to Jerusalem (Luke 19:1–10).

As a "chief tax collector" (verse 2), Zacchaeus was probably the main tax worker on the major trade route that passed through Jericho. He probably negotiated with the Roman government for the right to collect taxes, then farmed out this work to other tax agents. The system was noted for its fraudulent practices, and it likely made Zacchaeus a wealthy man.

Zacchaeus had probably heard about Jesus's acceptance of tax collectors and other sinners. He wanted only to get a glimpse of Jesus, the miraculous healer and teacher, as He passed by. But Jesus surprised Zacchaeus by calling him down from his perch in a sycamore tree. Then Jesus invited himself to the tax collector's home.

This encounter with Jesus was a life-changer for Zacchaeus. He promised to repay fourfold those people whom he had cheated. As further evidence of his change of heart, Zacchaeus vowed to give half of his possessions to the poor.

Jesus was quick to forgive this taxman-turned-philanthropist and welcome him into God's kingdom. Might Jesus have been surprised by this strong show of faith and evidence of repentance? After all, the Lord himself had earlier declared, "It is easier for a camel to go through the eye of a needle than for someone who is rich to enter the kingdom of God" (Luke 18:25). Perhaps, after this encounter, Jesus's steps were a little lighter as He resumed His journey toward Jerusalem. See also *Tax Collector.*

ZEALOTS. In New Testament times, a party of fervent Jews who opposed the rule of Rome over their homeland. They were willing to fight to the death to restore Jewish independence. Jesus's disciple called Simon the Zealot may have been a member of this sect, or he may have believed in its principles. See also *Simon the Zealot.*

ZECHARIAH. A godly priest presiding at the altar when the angel Gabriel told him he would become father of the forerunner of the Messiah. Zechariah found this hard to believe, since he and his wife were childless and too old to bear children (Luke 1:5–22).

Because of his doubt, Zechariah was punished with an inability to speak during his wife Elizabeth's pregnancy. Imagine how he must have wanted to tell everyone who would listen that this old couple was expecting a miracle son!

At the appointed time, the child was born. Several members of Zechariah's extended family suggested the child be named for his father. But Elizabeth insisted the baby would be known as John, in obedience to the instructions of the angel Gabriel. Since Zechariah couldn't speak, he took a tablet in hand and wrote, "His name is John" (Luke 1:63).

Immediately Zechariah was able to speak and broke out in a song of praise to God, who was preparing the way for the redemption of His people (Luke 1:68–79). See also *Benedictus*; *Elizabeth*; *John the Baptist.*

Z

Enjoy this book? Help us get the word out!

Share a link to the book or
mention it on social media

Write a review on your blog, on a retailer site,
or on our website (dhp.org)

Pick up another copy to share with someone

Recommend this book for your
church, book club, or small group

Follow Discovery House on
social media and join the discussion

Contact us to share your thoughts:

 @discoveryhouse   @DiscoveryHouse

Discovery House
P.O. Box 3566
Grand Rapids, MI 49501 USA

Phone: 1-800-653-8333
Email: books@dhp.org
Web: dhp.org